Reflections in Poems and Songs

Different Every Time, Never Twice the Same

Reflections in Poems and Songs
Different Every Time, Never Twice the Same

Ally Shearer

ATHENA PRESS
LONDON

Reflections in Poems and Songs
Different Every Time, Never Twice the Same
Copyright © Ally Shearer 2007

All Rights Reserved

ISBN 10-digit: 1 84748 000 4
ISBN 13-digit: 978 1 84748 000 2

First Published 2007 by
ATHENA PRESS
Queen's House, 2 Holly Road
Twickenham TW1 4EG
United Kingdom

Printed for Athena Press

For Annette, Arvo and Erin

Most grateful thanks to:

Flora MacCrae for patience personified and exemplary help in the preparation of this work.

The Hamiltons of Eastcote for their devotion to the culture.

The two Ian Muirs – Prestwick and Hungerford, along with Sandy Nixon, Colin Dewar, Chris Walker and Kate Sandeman. Modern greats and much-valued friends.

Piper Alan Paterson. Scottish Borders and Melbourne Australia for generosity, courage and bearing – after all.

The Mortons of Ayrshire.

Karin Ingram (editor) of Hawick. For fine publication.

Gilly Austin of Guildford, Surrey, England. For over twenty-three years of never-confusing friendship with personal gain.

If you meet someone without a smile,
give them one of yours.
(A life motto)

Ally Shearer

Canto I, Stanza I

The stag at eve had drunk his fill,
Where danced the moon on Monan's rill,
And deep his midnight lair had made,
In lone Glenartney's hazel shade;
But when the sun his beacon red
Had kindled on Benvorlich's head,
The deep-mouthed bloodhound's heavy bay
Resounded up the rocky way,
And faint, from farther distance borne,
Were heard the clanging hoof and horn.

Sir Walter Scott, The Lady of the Lake

Briagha, Mattie and Author

A Birthday Song for Mattie, Aged 9

Composed by Ally Shearer, 24 November 2003

There was Louie and there was me,
And some friends came round for tea,
As they tumbled through the door
There was lots of room for more.

We had football, we had stuff
And at times we got so rough,
But the run that we all had
Showed my birthday wasn't bad.

Such a lovely day for me,
So surely you can see –
That as we played around
We all laughed so merrily.

Well we hopped and jumped around
Till we all fell on the ground,
And the bestest of all times
Is what my birthday party found.

A Celtic Thocht

Composed by Ally Shearer, Thursday, 11 August 2005.

Sica sair yer sorra set ye,
Man ye wyte – till Divil get ye –
A canna thole yon thing that frets ye –
Afore yer destinay!

A December Morn

Composed by Ally Shearer, 2 December 2005, at 1.30 a.m.
(Ally – with himself.)

Oh, how I love the light of dawn
That greets me in the frosty morn.
The blackbird in his search for food,
The 'woodie' not yet in the mood –
For him no breakfast execution,
Just simple female persecution.

As Phil and Jemima, the squirrel pair,
On feet so cold, tho' lots of hair –
Take pride of place, at table fair,
While robin and dunnock do stand and stare.

As the sky of pink and stripey red,
Light early planes up, overhead,
As I'm long-lifted from my bed,
No muddled worry in my head,
Just simple plan, I lay for me,
To keep the happy spirit free –
For my world around, and all to see.
And share the love that beckons me,
And gently welcome destiny…

Collated and manoeuvred before going to sleep – perchance to dream.
(Till early call – from Colin 'Traffic Control Pal' – The Mighty
O'Leary! – 'Colin-All-Cars'!)

A Dream of Ayr

Composed by Ally Shearer, Wednesday, 8 November 2006.

I dreamed a dream, a dream so fair –
That I did stroll in the town of Ayr,
I saw a kirk, the first one there;
On a cushion kneeled guid Will Adair
A detailed scene, sae fine and rare,
Was the dream I dreamed – o' the Toon o' Ayr.

A Doggone Poem

Tuesday, 18 November 2003, early a.m.

The weekend buzz, all gone,
She sits there part forlorn,
Parted from her Daddy there on Monday,
From her kennels she was took,
No time to read a buke –
For it's doggone home,
And every day is fun day,
'*Ard Choille* – aargh!'
To the hills and briars once more
And to meet old friends galore – 'Yap-yap!' – sniff and
   run…

A 'Happy Man' Thought

Composed by Ally Shearer, 20 January 2005.

Noo a hombre wi' a dog
Can be a happy man.
Young ones gone, wifie too,
No need for a pram...
Just to walk the fields o' Ashridge,
Is as bliss, 'as happy can'.
Jist dog an' me an' a flask o' tea,
Yes – I'm a happy man.

A Kidwelly Frien'
(A Fairmer Pal – in West Wales)

Composed by Ally Shearer, Drumshang, Scotland, 22 December 2006, at 7 p.m.

Devoted and besotted – is a dog attached tae me,
Reminds me o' a fairmer in Welsh Wales by Kid-wellee,[*]
I mind the day I met him he was standin' like a stook,
His hobby Summer's evenin', wis jis-tae-stand and look –
As the big red sun sinks in the West,
Meanderin' thoughts wi' time he's got,
Are what he loves the best.

For holidays he'd wynd his way –
Across to County Clare –
Tae dance and sing, till rafters ring,
So oft-times he was there,
I ast'im the attraction – his truth forthcomin' rare,
Tol' me of how, he takes his bow,
At the annual Spinsters' Fair.

We parted in guid company – till another time we met.
In car park handed me his card,
(I thought) No need for a vet!
The card said, *You can hire a bull, Kidwelly is the place…*
But where I live in London town, I'd hardly have the space…
And I fondly do remember, that smile upon 'iz face!

---

[*] Kidwelly.

The folk we meet along the street could never be the same.
They only see the pavin' steins, when they do scurry hame.
Their routine life – their toil and strife – *their* momentary
  gain,
My Toil and Tears, of fifty years – and yet I'm glad I came;
But youthful days and 'Kidwelly Ways', will aye remain the
  same.

Alive – All the Time
(For the man already outside his skin, tho' not his mind)

*Composed by Ally Shearer, Wednesday, 25 January 2006, at 1 a.m.
(on Burns' 'mourning').*

So here I bide – not nearly dead,
Worldly wise – and I've been fed,
Can o' beans – an' a loaf o' bread,
So I am quite contented…

The story hasn't yet been read,
Regardless o' what mony said,
Nae need the 'Moguls' get excited –
Ah havenae yet… sat doon tae write it.

Obit-u-aries – are not much fun,
So I'll do mine, afore I'm done,
The fame and fortune I've acquired,
Is more than I at first desired;
But if I've pleasured – some – or few –
I've earned the right tae a tale or two.
And the best is tae come, and at last ye'll laugh,
Wi' my epi-taph – in the *Tele-graph*!
'Boom boom!'
They'll hae some fun…

In part inspired (halfway through) by the 'Pooch Wyn' man (it's
affa teuch at the top), Upper Tullig, Kilflyn, Co. Kerry, Eire.*

*And Donal' Stuart o' the 'forty pooches' in Aberdeenshire! – in the
Tinker's Tartan! Long ago! – wi' his dochter, Mary – on her bike
encircling the lad before snatchin' his 'Piece and Jam', scoffing it… and
flingin' the crust o'er the bushes!*

---

* Circa 1970, apparently.

19

All Around and Round
(A Love Song)

Lyrics by Ally Shearer, 21 May 2005.
For the tune 'Dorothy and Angus Ogston's Waltz', by R McCombie.

All round and round we go,
A sweetheart to find,
I see you more now,
Always on my mind,
Oft-times I think of you,
When I'm all alone,
You feel how I feel,
We should both be one.

Some say the world is wrong,
Giving such as we,
But the world goes round, love.
Surely they can see,
Maybe all our dreams
Vanish with the wind.
Will our love return,
So that we'll begin again.

Repeat first verse.

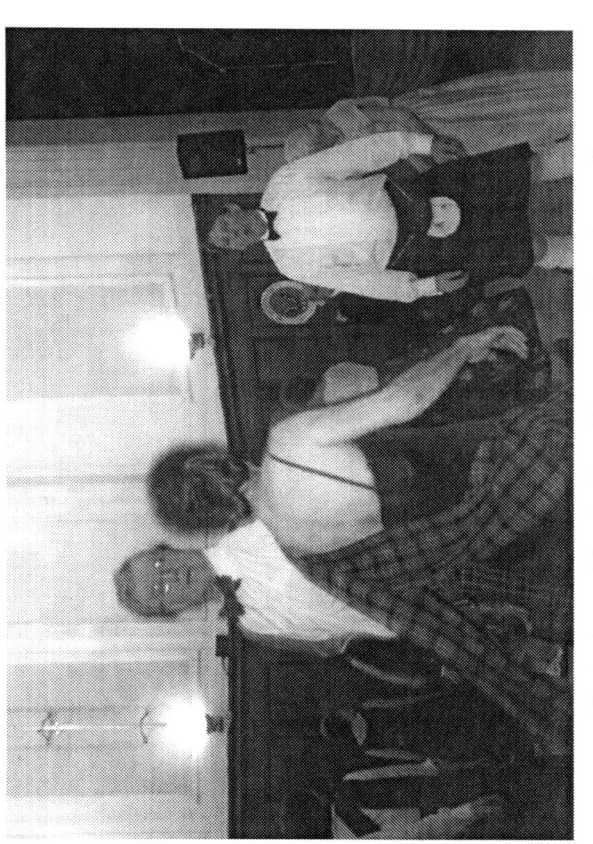

The Author and friends. Friend Brian says 'What about me?'
Berkhamsted Strathspey and Reel Club, 51st Annual Highland Ball, Ashlyns, Herts – January 2003

All Around the Floor

Lyrics by Ally Shearer, 23 May 2005.
For the tune 'Stuart and Lena's Golden Wedding Waltz', by
Rob McCombie.

So hullo – tae you, and you, and tae you, and you and you,
It's only me that you can see,
I've been away, as I say tae you, and you.
Here's a fine how do ye do,
I'm telling you, there's little more,
That I can say,
I accept for you, and you,
No longer feeling blue.
I've seen so much to do,
Along the way.
So if you will pardon me,
Hing aroon, so I can see.
If you'll be here, alang wi' me,
To end the day.

Here we go round and round and all around,
Friends all on the floor.
Dancing all as one, it seems,
We'll be here for more,
Gold – in life I've had along with you,
All along the way,
So darling now it often seems,
We both are here alone to stay.

Repeat first verse.

Ally and Flora's Hogmanay Waltz

Presented to them, the arrangers of the above, by the composer Rob McCombie, of Ruthven Brae, Aboyne, on the occasion of Bill Black's Hogmanay night at Banchory 2005/2006.

Composer: Rob McCombie.
Lyrics by Ally Shearer; arranged by Ally Shearer and Flora McCrae. Song.

We all came home to be alone,
And set our spirits soaring free,
The New Year time was yours and mine,
And made for you and me.
So to roam no more by foreign shore –
And be where Scottish hearts belong;
So to peace and joy, we will employ,
And this will be our song.

Music, two lines.

These foreign lands, however grand,
Could never be like home to me,
And I will go with hearts that know,
Where eagles fly so free.
So let us roam, our Highland Hills once more,
The Glenside Burn that ripples still,
And McCombie's ways will still amaze,
And set our hearts on trill.

Repeat last four lines.

Ally's Only Rap No.

On an Ally wake-up at 5.30 a.m., with words for rap composed by Ally Shearer, Friday, 4 November 2005.

Wid yow table-top duds and yu Rastaman hair,
Yow al' turn up and yu lookin' fo' a chair,
It's yo go, go here and yo go, go thay,
Ya gonna do ya thing and ya doin' owkay,
Yuh gonna hav' de rum, and it ain't off tap,
Ye waggle up and down, and ye doin' de Rap!
Mon you doin' some good and ye ain't 'aff bad,
Ye go indinmon, an' ye doin' de trad.

Chorus:

In ya hip-hop shoe, an' ya table-top wrap,
Ye doin' de dance an' ye ain' half krap – 'Yeh, Mon!'
In yo' hip-hop shoe and yu doo-vay wrap,
Ye doin' de ting and ye ain' half krap – 'Yeh, Mon!'

Wait na' neva-min'-yu-yap,
No mo' ding-dong, no Anglo-feeli' krap,
Jus' do ya ting and a-singin' yow Rap,
Wid yow yella-red shoes and yu table'cloff wrap,
Jus' dissy yo dance and yo doin' lyke dat!

Chorus, as above.

Ya neva' myn' yu yap, no yu Anglo-feeli' krap,
Jus' do ya ting an' de body down flat – 'Yeh, Mon!'
If ye gel don' do she wanna, lie down flat –
She can cling on de chair, an' jus' get fat –
She can cling on de chair, an' jus' get fat –
'Jus'-lyke dat – jus'-lyke dat!'

A Love's Lost Dream

Composed by Ally Shearer, Sunday, 11 June 2006, in London.

Do you recall, that fondest kiss,
In thon December hall?
Conveyed to Southern Hemisphere
No leaden weight at all,
Where healing time I sought to gain,
When failed the Spanish shore,
New Zealand's end to end sublime,
Alone I did explore.

Two decades on, all time forgone
Since meeting you again,
Poor copy of yon teenage love,
Recalled as ever when
Fond vision, golden of your tress.
Smile, demure and slow
That's turned true hearts of gentlemen,
To those as cold as snow.

Past times gone – all mastered some
Wi' pay cheque signs removed,
Ten years of fond rehearsal;
Some million hearts now soothed.
Lives there a man – with brain to scan,
Some work of honour see,
Believes in life, still lived in –
Not posthumous-ly!

Could such a man, whose judgement clear,
Watch others teach the course to steer?
Yet runs himself, life's maddening rave –
Stand – paused – without a tear –
Surveying such a grave!

And so: were 'Millbrae Vennel' up for sale,
Blithe spirit yield tae; most,
There as a squatter, I'd be found,
All rite and sight be lost
When Robbie's Genius spirit flew.
At speed unheard by most,
To join the waiting Angels,
And meet his Holy Ghost.

NB1: A farewell to the love of this life then.

NB2: Burns' fine house in Dumfries referred to: Millbrae Vennel.

NB3: One part in a line in stanza four refers to 21 July 1796. Also included in miniscule part, in stanza three, some clue as to my own personal 'has-been' job – like that of 'RB' – which couldn't change one's natural personality; nevertheless, in several areas, was equally antisocial and demanding of the necessary dull negativity, of the boring time 'needs-spent' in covert situ.

A Man Called Billy

Composed by Ally Shearer, 14 February 2005.

'Foreword':

'In the dreichy days o' Winter, wi' rain and hail and storm –
'Twas Billy Connolly's wit we had, to keep our spirits warm.'

In the early 'daze', all in a haze, still wondrin' who I am –
Cam' news o' one, 'twas said to be – anither kind o' man.
So, fuelled wi' curiosity, I made a trip to town –
Got off at old Victoria, nearby the underground.

I'd booked my seat, no one to meet
Just me – and my info' found.
And soon I laughed my sides off, as that man walked all
    around.
Wi' Fyffe banana boots on, he strutted out his form,
On a stage the size o' Hampden Park, the moment he
    stood on.
In awe I sat there all entranced, as my Celtic heart it
    danced,
To the strains upon a banjo – you could hear across in
    France.

Noo years have passed since '84; George Orwell's been and
    gone,
But the 'Big-Yin' they called 'Billy', just goes for ever on.
And it's really guid for Billy too – he wisnae just a poet –
His fun does echo round the world, the roars o' laughter
    show it!

And so – guid on ye Billy lad, ignoring all they said,
Wi' their nanny goat intelligence – before they up and fled.
They don't prefer the poem that rhymes, without a backcloth
  snap –
That simply helps them comprehend, some *'intellectual
  krap'*.

*[NB: That's like 'common-speak' for stuff too highbrow for bairns and
humble folk.]*

So here's to the 'absurdity' of geniuses like Burns,
And seldom seen in plaid, and sometimes known to scorn.
For now the view of Billy, is scattered far and wide,
His courage says what others think, and how they may deride.

And – so Billy Lad – re early 'daze'
Wi' the bubble burst – on a bran' new craze
Ye paid no mind tae the things they said
The low IQs and the nearly dead...
Those mindless wannabies, in their Sunday suits,
The 'must go and sees' tae 'discover their roots'.
I've seen them a' frae boy tae man
I knew I was different – I never had a pram!
And now the time to pass has come,
When their daily doze o' intellect – scoots oot 'their (b.b.)
  other end'.

A Minute in the Mornin'

Composed by Ally Shearer, Sunday, 12 February 2006.
On seeing a Sunday Post *picture of Rommel's bunker for Hitler.*

This is a gentle wee poem!

Noo Hitler was a bastard,
As everyone agrees,
Wi' a passion for destruction,
Baith at hame and overseas;
Ower busy makin' bullets,
Tae tak notice o' the trees,
A michty man was Adolf,
Bringin' nations to their knees,
But wis feenish'd in a hell-hole…
Noo wisn't *that* a wheeze!

Among the Carrick Hills

Composed by Ally Shearer, 23 January 2006.
Tune adaptation: D Flat Major, 3/4 steady.
Song.

I just received a letter, from my home on Ayr-toon strand,
That scribble so familiar in my Mother's feeble hand,
The voice that rang with music, and with laughter now is
  still:
'*Dear Ally, it's so lonely now, among my Carrick Hills…*'

Up one octave.

As I gaze across the ocean, I relive a moment's joy,
The moorlands and the meadows, where I rambled as a
  boy,
The photo when I left her then, is by my bedside still:
'*Dear Ally, it's so lonely now, among my Carrick Hills…*'

*Solo band in verse one, and to raise key in ?E Flat Major and
repeat last line to last verse repeat.*

An April Sunday Morning, 2006

Composed by Ally Shearer, 23 April 2006.

An April sunny morning, beneath a hawthorn tree,
There's a peace and soft serenity which has enraptured me,
The sound of winging kittywake, the bowing woodland
dove,
Brings close to me the Heaven, they proclaim is high
above.

Since first I travelled wearily from London's grimy south,
Thinking of my Highland youth, warm smile did grace my
mouth,
But landed then in Ayrshire, 'mang the hames o' Robbie
Burns,
The memory soon got flooded, wi' rhyming verse return.

Romantic thought, tho' never sought, supplied by sight
and sound,
Ten thousan' mile – a winsome smile – may staunch the
turnaround.
But long established mystery, that haunts the lonely heart –
Who should decree of he and she, the sweetest love to
part?

To never meet remains so sweet, sometimes a kind repose,
Till tiny glance in happenstance, the jagged heart suppose;
And so return to early days with skylarks rising high.
Before we ever witnessed 'Coastguard' 'copters in the sky.

The 'hundred-mile-an-hourers' that race along the glen,
As the curlew and the corncrake, are reduced to whisper
   then,
The rhythmic passing cormorant seems sore obliged to
   flee,
Just like the time, once yours and mine, and babes upon
   the knee.

What of this speed, and what's the need, to change most
   everything?
Let's fix the potholes and the drains – afore 'Eagles' start to
   sing!
Do they, like me, still try to see the beauty that is there,
As they switch us off, like the lever swung – on an execution
   chair?
In 'my' time left, I'm warning them – of a future grim:
   Beware!

Aneth the Flite-path
'No Deid Yet'

Composed by Ally Shearer, Thursday, 21 October 2005, at 5 a.m.

Och, Ah've risen up again.
And the blue skies fu' o' planes.
An' the sun is shining brightly,
This fine morning.
So Ah'm ringing o'er tae you,
An' my belly's feeling fu'
For draft purridge is no thing
That they'll be scornin'.

Music: 6/8 time or e.g. 'Echty Street in Glesca', 2/4 time.

An Ode to the 'Youth Time'
(I Might As Well)

Begun early 2002; second attempt 4 June 2002; relocated 20 March 2004. NB: Jotted, as I recall, in the dark.

I've never had the chance
To sow an apple or a rose.
Or be content with what I know,
It's too late, I suppose,
To lift this corn-sack off my back.
And leave this weary drill.
Then simply saunter home alone,
And think about you still…

So I might as well be home alone,
As oft-times done before,
I might as well, like 'Auld Lang Syne',
Lean agin' an open door,
With empty satisfaction.
As I wander round and round,
Just knowing in my heart of hearts,
You're nowhere to be found.

Another Ode to Life

Composer: Ally Shearer, 2 March 2003.
(Adapted.)

There's always another tomorrow,
However hard the day,
There's always an end to sorrow,
Time wipes our tears away.
There's always a reason for living,
Though sad the heart may be,
There's always another horizon.
Beyond the one we see...

Why so? – Well... there's crocuses, for a start –

They peep through the earth.
Snowdrops dance on lawns.
Lovely signs of rebirth – of Spring
Now that Winter's gone,

So we can be – like those sweet flowers
That brighten up the ground,
And smile through the sunshine showers,
Spreading joy around.

A Peaceful Christmas Time

Composed by Ally Shearer, 24 December 2005
by Arbuthnott, The Mearns, Aberdeenshire.

Clear half-mune present, and the Ploo' aye there,
First light of dawn and free of care,
No screeching cock pheasant rends the air –
But the michty black grouse – at least four pair!

My! But the peace that fills the air,
Nae 'Niagra traffic' or else, to rin and tare,
Dog stock still, as she sniffs at the snare:
Will we ever more see the proud white hare?

Christmas Eve ready for the young folks' thrill,
Tiny lights twinkle on yonder hill,
Irreplaceable times to fear no ill.
And the 'sunshine' of childhood to smile on – still.

Met cousin Dodie, and it's Betty next,
A dozen gran' weans will teach me the text,
Nae doot in their time, they'll move up a gear,
Efter a' fits it a' aboot? – It's just another year.
Bring-on-the-dance, o' Life's Big Whurlaroon',
Like the skirl o' the pipes – they'll mak their ain soond.

And us that are left – wi' time unspent,
Who'll quietly watch – all that Heaven sent,
Plenty tae do, plenty tae mind,
Rewards of life – more easy to find,
No need movin' on tae pastures new,
And plenty time left for the Me and the You.

A Pre-dawn Chorus Tribute

Composed by Ally Shearer, 16 January 2006 (twixt 3.50 and 4.51 a.m.).

I rumble around with sleeping all done;
The juggernauts keep rolling by,
From the roaring M1 and the night-time sky.
But I hear from my cot, and calm sublime,
The chorus of 'life' pays no heed of time –
And the music and song, from birds of all name,
Forty or so, from a thrush in the main.
Soon I must depart, from affairs of the heart,
Aye happy to meet – more sorry to part,
From music and verse once more I must flee,
Back to ol' London, the rush and melee.
Churn the old dirge, and down with the pen,
Problems to solve for women and men,
But I won't stick it long – I'll return in a while,
To another *comeback* – and I'll do it in style.

Sat silent with dog during extraordinary dawn chorus.

Ard Choille
(High Wood)

For Robert (Rob) Roy MacGregor.

Composed by Ally Shearer; commenced in September sunshine on the 28th, 2005, and completed at 1 a.m., 3 December 2006.

Dog at heel, o'er mountain crag,
In downwind sight o' grouse and stag.
Far from invasion's stoney shore –
Hame at last, to leave no more.

Wha delivered me this place –
O' peaceful hue and flowering grace –
If I could clasp the michty haun,
Bestowed tae me, sic Native Land.

Ere I depart my Heilan' tread,
Let no man deem it to be said,
In that place, brave *Wallace* bled;
Was there no spot – to lay my head?

For recognised by friend or foe –
Time is come, and I must go –
Back to my land o' Hill and Glen –
Sweet Silver Rivers – speak my name.

Done and dusted!

Quote: Breathes there a man with soul so dead, who never to himself hath said, 'This is my own my Native Land!'?

NB: Ard Choille *is the Gaelic MacGregor 'War Cry'. One can see at a glance, therefore, the* shrewd *significance.*

A Shepherd's Love

Composed by Ally Shearer, 31 August 2002; rearranged 22 January 2004.
Tune adapted from 'Mattie's Birthday Song', 23 November 2003.
G Major.

I've been roamin' all around,
But you know I've never found,
Another smile as sweet as yours.
That I can treasure all the while.
From the Highlands to Carlisle,
They'll never capture that winsome smile:
Where have you been, my pretty queen –
The like of you I've never seen?

Tune varies.

Some folk like me and you, are not the best –
With fancy words, like all the rest,
Some broken hearts can never mend,
It's no use to just pretend,
Heaven knows if I had found
Happiness with you around,
Or was it just another fling,
Another time to dance and sing?

Band in four lines then repeat, 'Some folk like me…' etc.

A Simple Existence in October Tour
'Mid Bonnie Ayrshire's Autumn

Composed by Ally Shearer, 30 October 2006.

Well, now that I'm here, some plans are laid –
Cementing things that'll never fade –
It's a gladdening fortune, that's never wrang –
Which brought the views from sweet 'Drumshang'.
Sublime are the times I've roved around here,
Winters and Summers and Easters clear,
To back in my time – when I knew no fear,
And present days full of surprises:
'Doggies' and owners, all shapes and sizes.

In a tiny 'shebeen' near the town of Ayr,
A six-foot wall, with no inch to spare
At rosettes in their hundreds, I stand and stare,
At the huge blaze of colour – before me there.
And so much to follow, a wee girl's parade,
Crufts a whole world over, a labour of love
Not just the one – called *Rover*.

Distractions again, often confessed
As I've ducked and dived and worked with the best,
A million 'belly-laughs' and countless times digressed
A bush for each gap, a value I learned
The reaction found to joys well earned.
So I take my reward, as I walk with the tide
In the Autumn sun, with dog alongside,
Just grateful for health and the guid folk I meet
For I know life fulfilled – and there's plenty that's sweet.

A Soldier's Lass

Composed by Ally Shearer, 12 January 2006.
Tune: G Major – adapted.

Such a long way from Basra, so far to come home,
They have sent my poor darling to another time zone;
The whole ugly war that has happened again,
Why does it happen again and again?

Music, one line.

So my sweetheart went off to the war all alone,
Just myself and our young one left here by the phone,
There is nowhere to call and no one to come home,
What becomes of the ones who are left here alone?

Music, one line; or repeat last two lines, inc. vocal then music,
one line.

'Twas only last Christmas, we went to the Ball,
May we go there again – have you time to recall?
Och the Black Watch are best with their backs to the wall:
Will you come home again – will you come home at all?

For waltzers on the floor: Band in now whole o' the verse to
modulate up-key for vocalist verse two – repeat, and also repeat
last line, viz: 'What becomes of…' etc.

Arrange to suit.

A Statement by a Humble Country Poet

1 May 2005, at 3.30 a.m.

So-called 'Poems' of centuries past, which are reminiscent of writings of non-rhyming stanzas of today, in total contradiction to 'Poetry' as defined by the *Oxford English* and *Collins Dictionaries*.

Found in readings during time spent in peace and tranquility around the donkey sanctuaries of e.g. St Boswells by Melrose, Scotland, Sidmouth, East Devon, and Hertfordshire, England.

A woman observing the Springtime of another era long ago, writes a 'poem' of these lovely times in the idiom, some would say 'idiotic', of the e.g. pseudo-intellectual non-rhyming stuff, still seen and published in e.g. the wonderful old *Scots Magazine* of today. In any case, all of it is so unlike my personal three years or so to date of happy rhymings; thus far turned down for publication by some.

I must say that – as the following is just a personal observational statement – it may verge on the controversial, although the occasional 'speak-easy' debate has never satisfied the mystery for me. However, no offence intended and so it goes:

The aftermentioned here is a humble rhyming poet's example of how it once was accepted poetry in days long gone by. A rich lady once wrote and published such 'happy' stuff as the following. Obviously she left heirs to follow her. I quote:

To what purpose, April, did you return again?
Beauty is never enough.
You can no longer quiet me with redness
Of little leaves, opening stickily,
I know what I know,
The sun is hot on my neck, as I observe the spikes of the crocus.
The smell of the earth is good.

Her poem appears to go downhill from here, and hardly with the joys of Spring! But when does the Poetry begin?

It is apparent, that there is no death.
But what does that signify?
Not only underground are the brains of men eaten by maggots.
Life in itself is nothing – an empty cup,
A flight of uncarpeted stairs,
It is not enough that yearly, down this hill,
April comes like an idiot, babbling and strewing 'flowers'.

Am 'I' missing something – or is it them, after all… and even yet? Surprising for me, as it was to read such scratchings and deliberate opinion, from observations, by some person long before our time, declaring, in the idiom of today, that which some call poetry. Better to be alive in all the senses. I feel I rest my case and – maybe immoveable as I am – my suitcase!

A Tale of Moved Along Love

A poem and song by Ally Shearer 3/4 time in F Major, 23 June 2003
With verse one as the chorus, repeated with the variations.

Well, how have you been
Since the last time we met?
The like of you seldom seen...
It is little wonder that I can't forget
Happy days when you were my queen.

The lanes that we rambled.
The dances we knew,
I imagine we're goin' there still,
From the river vale yonder.
Down sweet shady rill.
For me there was no one like you.

Chorus: 'So how have you been...'

Has your life moved along
Through pastures all new?
While mine hasn't moved on at all,
Has your story been told,
Is there yet some to tell,
Will you ever make sense of it all?

(Music, one line – suggest) into chorus: 'And how are you
now...' *Band in – four lines or so.*

Will Spring come again to our valley below?
Will heaven be restored once again?
Will our heav'n be somewhere…
We already know
Are we only in dreams now and then?

Chorus: 'So how are you…' *Move key up to G Minor.*

A Thought for Fiddle Player, the Late Sean McGuire

Composed by Ally Shearer, 12 December 2004, at midnight.
A Poym in Rhyming Verse / Then awa tae ma bed…

Sae here's tae you,
Wi' comely hue,
An' here's tae you wi' knobs on!
More power tae you, for what ye do –
An elbi' grease that rubs on.

'The them' that said that you were dead,
And them that aren't in it,
Wi' precious little in their head –
An' canna play or sing it.

Their length an' breadth and travel wide,
Their Simmer heat an' wise-cool…
Their knowledge *can* the world deride.
Upon a local bar stool.

But what of legacy, well worthwhile,
And talent true abounding –
What e'er it be, in prose or style –
Like a Mozart score resounding.

From what fine head has it been said,
A brain to know no rust,
'Quoth' talent can do, as talent can,
But genius'll do what it must.

Auchiries School
The Hazy Days of Summer Hols

Penned by Ally Shearer, 29 March 2004, at HH.

Abune thon Hill O' Benachie – 'mid scope and glen and
  bracken free,
We'd guddle eels, scale fallen tree – Andy, Dod, Bill and
  me…

On river large we'd cast oor nets, and puddle aroon in
  rivulets –
The screech at a 'find', the joy sublime – Time on our
  hands – Och, never you mind.

No fear nor care in hearts so young; huge rubbish dumps –
  'things' to be found.
The auld tin kettle and robin's nest; we'd riches untold to
  beat the rest.

Oor hoose in the clouds – abune the world – and no way
  back – 'till a rope unfurled,
As when hunger struck wi' a belly pang – explaining to do
  – an' it wunna be lang.

The orchard'll wait – till next fun time, for I now just
  heard the toon clock chime.
We'll trudge awa hame, wi' our new-found find, and hide
  oor stash till yokin time.

Trudging hame, gin' lousin' time – another verse could
  mend this rhyme.
Had we been good frae three till nine? – Tomorrow's film
  night for loon and quine.

But first it's 'Ally, get up!' there's neeps tae pu' and hens
tae feed and drain the coo' –
Cat's mewin' as they catch the drips – the next episode
could have you in fits.

Meanwhile, suffice for you to know, corn to turn and hay
to stow;
Then of course the horse, or didn't you know?
It's well past seven and there's school tae go.

Through Kennedy's yard and the 'bubbilee-Jox', there's
danger afoot as I pull up my socks.
There's a six-foot gate for me to face, and a 'futterin'
cockerel for me to race.

Then to classroom Auchiries we hae returned, for twa lang
weeks as the heather burned,
Nae mair wark, by Geordie's midden – wi' bikes and
school books – a' bit hidden.

Nae 'bannox' or scone – and certain' nae soda –
As Dominie cries, 'Ony mair Coka Rhoda?'

Tonight it's the film, we'll run if we can, 'Hop Along
Cassidy' was my 'Champion man' –
Shot to bits near every week, turns up brand new a'
trousered and sleek.

Then hame again, through the Summer's eve' haze, for
there's teuchits, curlews and skylarks to raise,
A' back-hame-tae-normal on Benachie' s braes – 'twas hazy
and lazy – but those were the days.

*Gee! Thanks for comin' back wi' me – it's been humbling. Cheerio
the noo.*

With Cousin Rhoda – Methven, Perthshire

A Wee Chorus to Climate Change

Composed by Ally Shearer, 16 October 2006.

A 'magnolian' daffodil December, oranges in Spring,
This is the song I have foretold, the English folk will sing.

Just one certain 'soon to be' – an Ally Shearer prophecy.

Ayrtoun – Yett?

Is the Gate of Ayr as open as e.g. the Gaiety Theatre?

Composed by Ally Shearer, 30 November 2006, St Andrew's Day, at 1 a.m.

So here I am in 'Ayrtoun',
This Blessing by the sea,
Friendly folk, kindly folk,
Have already greeted me.
I remember well my first time there,
It really warmed the heart.
And when I came to live in it,
Was sorry for to part.

If you have been away like me,
For many a 'long gone year' –
You'll know the depth of loneliness,
That can't prevent the tear.
Engaged in lands beyond the sea
'Pervades' the Celtic heart –
At last the one thing left undone
'Return to the start'...

So here I am on bended knee,
Though humble, not forlorn –
To be where I am meant to be,
A Crake Amang the Corn –
Content as any pig in it,
This place whar 'Rab' was born.
Ah'll nestle doon, an 'Ayrtoun Loon' –
An' Ah'll start the Morra' Morn – *at last*!

Ally Shearer. Out of Aberdeenshire.

The town of Ayr from the Carrick hills

Back to 'Sligo
A Personal Ode to the 'Futility of War'

13 March 2003

I travelled back that I might see, your name upon the
stone;
The silence there that beckoned me, showed I was not
alone.
The river tumbling down and round, beneath the roadway
still.
'Who's that I see?' – a boy like me – at play amid the swirl.

I strolled through winding pathways, 'mid flowers and
buzzing bees –
I stood alone – though not alone – beneath the bowing
trees –
'Mid music of the silence, was no one there but me?
Then came upon the Celtic stone, upraised for all to see:
Your *name* so clear – 'John Simpson Dear' – to spare
someone like me.

Some folk did view the stranger's stance, the vigil plain to
see; of *final chance* –
Returned to glance, for all *eternity*!
The trembling feel, the piper's peal, so still, inside of me –
These forty years not wasted now that I am close to thee –
Dear Uncle John, though you're long gone, you're here
again with me;
For we are saved, by those who braved the *Hell* of History.

Ally Shearer – In Living Memory – 'Living In Memory': Winter
overhead / Spring essentially in my heart.

FOR REMEMBRANCE

1939	—	1945

THOMAS DUNN
JAMES JAFFRAY
WILSON LEDINGHAM
JOHN MALCOLM
WILLIAM NORRIE
SYDNEY PHILIP
JOHN SHEARER
RONALD SIMPSON
JOHN TAYLOR
WILLIAM STEWART

JAMES CREIG
WILLIAM JOHNSTONE
ANDREW MACKIE
WILLIAM MATHERS
JAMES PATERSON
ALEXANDER ROSS
JOHN SIMPSON
GEORGE STRACHAN
JOHN WATT
JOHN CARVOCK

Two Uncles-Simpson and one Uncle-Shearer. Names 'I waited' fifty years to see

Bancyfelin, Kidwelly – 'Uwern-in!'

Composed by Ally Shearer, 26 and 29 September 2006, Welsh Wales.

(To my first solo Sunday sojourn – 'Celtic Camping' in truly Welsh Wales.)

Climbed and walked up *Cam Widi* (Widdie) to see the
    silver sea,
Then beat it to the nearest caff for barmbrack (*brith*) and
    tea,
Soon scaled the heights of Penberrie, beneath a bright blue
    sky,
Then wint like 'hell' to Penny's Place – for steak and
    kidney pie.

The morrow I'll hope to observe the seas, all foaming
    white in splendour,
But if it rains, I'll just stay put – feet up on the fender.
Rain, gales and 'flood-some' wetter,
Yet – complexions anew, once more to view,
And by midweek, feeling better.

But before day three – to visit me –
Two tiny cats – all black,
Their spirited frolics, fun to see –
Now I'm glad that I came back.

This mighty sky, now rolling by,
Even the crows are heaven-sent,
And these undulating farmlands –
Huh – maybe it's home I went.

So this friendly Wales soon I must leave,
For now I've done my duty,
These loving folk I'll not forget,
And bring with me some beauty.

But now I gaze, thru' skylight's glaze,
And view the darkened hills, and farmlands without frills –
Then suddenly streams pure golden gleams,
Of 'our' star-shine cure of all ills – our sun – arising.

Beware of the ''Ru'
(Also recognised as the Kanga)

Probably for children, this one! So maybe if you could jist pretend.
Composed by Ally Shearer, 23 March 2006.

Noo if ever ye meet a 'ru, I'll tell ye what to do,
Fur he'll block yer route, that six-foot lout.
As yer face turns blue – and yer language too –
So prevention's the invention of 'sure', ye know,
Never confront a 'ru!

Anyway here's verse two about yon 'ru.

Like it's safe enough for a picnic lunch,
Way high up a eucalyptus branch.
For if the 'ru he lands a punch,
Ye'll know fine well you've been in a crunch,
Only for yer place on the high up bough,
Ye'd know well fine ye'd been in a row,
Sine yon 'Kuddly Bear' – that isn't a bear –
But a clawin' *mar-suppee-yil*,
He'll gie ye that stare, as he pulls oot yer hair,
An' the stink o't'l mak ye feel ill.

Noo a 'ru in a fight is a laffable sight –
Jist as lang as his opponent isn't you;
So never go 'Boo' tae the 'ru – jist find something safer tae
    do;
So as quick as ye like, get up on yer bike,
Get the hell oot o' sight o' that 'ru.
But if 'ru starts to jump, watch oot for yer rump,
For the 'ru is pure mean, thru' and thru'!
And – never try to be kind tae a 'ru; he'll never be kind tae
    you.

And – as sure as one and one's two – Ah'm stood here
tellin' you,
That 'ru's never been in a zoo!

NB: He's the absolute epitome o' belligerents!

*PS: A bit of a departure from my 'normal' things; and purely
intellectual stuff.*

Bluebell Time

Composed by Ally Shearer, 14 May 2006.
Song, D Major, 3/4 time.

Oh, the bluebells are blooming around my green glen,
I pause just to listen, to the magic, and then –
I can see your sweet face, and I'm happy again,
And again, and again, and again, and again.

The canopy high beech trees, swing in the breeze.
The 'ack-ack' green 'pecker resounds through the trees,
I can hear the first cuckoo go 'cuckoo' again,
And again, and again, and again, and again.

Ashridge Forest, Herts

Bonnie Doon, Dalrymple Way

Composed by Ally Shearer, Wednesday, 8 November 2006.

Did walk the day by Bonnie Doon,
Did balk and sway, her ben's aroon,
Her spray and swirl, her rapid birl –
No mountain rocks could smooth her;
An' 'Briagha' the dog, in joyous leap,
Found current, brown, too fierce, too deep,
And scrambled from the mighty spate.
For yin more second, be too late!
Sine 'drownded' dog would be her fate,
No man alive could soothe her.

Upstream we trudge, in sheer delight,
But must turn back before the night
Drops round us, like a darkening cloud,
Still rediscover and be proud;
See where the rushing Doon splits into three,
And fish-farm fish, no longer free –
Then a moment's ponder, as she separates,
Soliloquy for dinner plates;
Yet I'll visit more, this part of heaven
Should I survive, like Double-O-Seven.
Tho' despite clear blue and shiny sky,
No balustrade cuid quell nor pacify
The Mighty Doon I loved today
As I strode by Dalrymple Way.

The River Doon, Ayrshire in medium spate

Bonnie Glendevon

Composed by Ally Shearer, 12 October 2005.
Song, Waltz, Key D.

My Highland hills keep calling me,
Back to where I long to be,
With heather bells all greeting me,
Aroon by Aberfeldy.

Auchenblae might be the same,
And Teuchan braes still know my name,
By 'Devon's Glen the 'welcome hame' –
That's where I long to be.

Glendevon, Perth and Kinross

Bonnie Ina Campbell

For Erin Nicole Artna, daughter of Annette and Arvo

(A fun song about a little person, also fun for other little folk.)

Composed by Ally Shearer, 12 March 2005.
Key, D Major.

Chorus:

Now bonnie Ina Campbell, she's a glint upon her e'e;
She's sae bonnie Ina Campbell, I could dance her on my
    knee.
And the reason I refused her – you know she's only three,
And she's bonnie Ina Campbell with a glint upon her e'e.

Music, one line.

Now bonnie wee Ina Campbell when she comes to visit
    me,
She reads me poems and sings her song, as happy as could
    be
And the sun shines all the time, when she is standing next
    to me;
She's just bonnie Ina Campbell, and you know she's only
    three.

Music, two lines.
Chorus: 'Now bonnie Ina Campbell…' *etc.*

Well the reason I'm so happy now – as you can plainly
   see –
Is that bonnie Ina Campbell says she 'wants to marry me'.
But the reason I've refused her is, 'cause it can never be,
She's the dochter o' my dochter – and besides she's only
   three!

Music, one line.
Chorus: 'Now bonnie Ina Campbell…' *etc.*

Erin Artna of Orleans, Ontario. As 'Bonnie Ina Campbell'

Boxmoor Capers
(The Beauty and the Beasts)

An ode to Sunday, 10 September 2006.

*Composed by Ally Shearer; jotted on a train on Thursday, 14
September 2006, at 2.30 p.m.*
*Song/Poem – Proposed tune similar to 'Up went Nelson' (cudgelled).
Key, C/D.*

*(To be preceded by an emotional and true tale of the horses and their
wee foals, trapped by sheep wire in the middle of the 'River
Bulbourne', static and in fear.)*

We wint for a ramble – better than the sea.
Doon the wyndy river – jist Flurry, Dog and Me.
Where all kinds o' wildlife, surely you'll agree,
Better for the health, likewise the joie de vivre.

Music, one line.

Big dog Charlie's laffin' up at me.
Big girl Maisie climbin' up a tree.
Next thing a longhorn saunters up to see
Boxmoor capers in the mornin'.

Music, one line.

Then twa lanky-legged heron, baith standing in the burn,
In front o' forty seagulls, waitin' for their turn,
Sma' fish, big fish, none in vision yet,
In loups dog, becos-she-wanted-tae-get-wet.

Music, one line, Box and Mou' music.

Noo Charlie never knew till now, he could swim so well,
Briagha taught him how, becos she likes the smell,
Hard tae gar'em tae cum oot, so I jist said, 'Ach-tae-hell –
Wi' Boxmoor capers in the mornin'.'

Music, one line.

Then-'twis-like-a-thoosan'-mizzle-thrush lep'up fae the
    grass –
Gaed me sic a shock! – Ah nearly landed on my 'bottom'…
Syne they landed on the fence and I wish-I-cooda-cot'em.
Ah'd train that shower how to sing, because my singin's
    rotten.

Music, two lines.

There was twelve belted Galloway – moochin' in the
    watter –
Slurpin'-huge-pints-a'-draft-back – 'ziffit didnae matter,
Till byetrots the gelding, prood as he could be,
Twenty horseys follow him – headin' for their tea.

Music, one line.

See yon muckle willow there – where they'll all retire.
But happiness soon got me, when I saved them from the
    wire.

Repeat last line, ad-lib.

Re Performance: ref. At the beginning re the horses and the wire,
important to note the relevance in the last two lines!

Boxmoor capers

Braw Lads

Composed 20 August 2005 (Tempo like 'Phil the Fluter').

Noo there wiz Jimmy boy and Achi' boy fe' Aviemore and
   me,
Gan' up aroon and doon aroon the Hill a' Benachie,
There wis Bonnie loons and Ronnie loons and mony loons
   like me.
All fur oor health in the mornin'.

We wur tearin' a' aboot the place aroon the River Dee,
Divin' – dook ye couldna' look, sae deep ye couldna' see,
Met a funny man, fae up aroon Glenshee, said –
'Ah'm the Laird o' Udneys Feel, Fa's-Feel-are-ee.'

Wi' torn jeans and flingin' steins, so far's the eye could see,
Till Jimmy started greetin' and said, 'Ah've banged ma
   knee!'
But soon's the quines got landed, he wis richt as rain like
   me,
Sae good for oor health in the mornin'.

If sung, repeat verse one, e.g. 'Aye, there was Jimmy boy…' etc.

But Who Are You?

Composed by Ally Shearer, 18/19 June 2005; a midnight love song.

I just don't know what to do,
When I'd rather be with you,
As the sun comes shining through,
There is nothing left to do,
I've just got to go away.
Got to leave this very day,
There is nothing I can say,
You would hear now anyway.

Music to be composed.

By the Great Lochnagar
To Rob and Mary McCombie

Reviewed version of the original, 6 July 2005–27 February 2006.

Noo, I've traivilled that far tae the dark Lochnagar,
Thousan' miles for something to do,
A full hunder rhymes, and strife troubled times
A lad hairt-broke thru' and thru',
Aye – but ye'll know it's weel kent,
That when pitchin' my tent,
The road North wis aye something tae rue…
Though in peacetime or war, I wis never that far.
In my thoughts – fae the great Lochnagar,
And the thoughts that were mony, wi' the dreams to
    pursue,
Were of long winding roads, and of music by loads,
On my way back tae Mary and you…

I thankye baith in true frien'ship.

Cathkin Braes

Composed by Ally Shearer, Monday, 14 August 2006, at
10.40 a.m., Hemel Hempstead.
Key C.
(Addressed as more political than satire.)

Chorus:

Dinna hing yer claes by Cathkin Braes,
When dryin' is yer thinkin',
For below blue skies, there's a million flies,
And the Council tips are stinkin'.

Music, two lines.

Noo Glasgow refuse o' the toon,
Tho' residents won't know it –
They're garbage tonnage strewn aroon,
Where the Council waggons throw it.

Chorus – as above; music, one line.

Puir Jim the teacher and his lass,
Huv tried tae move beyon' it,
Thru' twenty-five years o' flies and tears,
But naebody wants tae know it.

Chorus – as above; music, two lines.

The 'Council Head' he sez –
'Teuch luck and it's I for one won't go there,
Those villages are where we sling oor muck,
What *they* really need, is snow there.'

Chorus – as above.
Repeat last two lines and ad-lib to fade.

Aberdeenshire – 'Mormon Braes'.
Scottish Traditional Tune – adapted.

Childhood Sweetheart
A Song to Maggie

Composed December 2003.
G Major, 3/4 time; last two line intro.

Oh I had a darlin' when I left my home,
Bound for the world for ever to roam,
I see her gold tresses twinkle so fine,
And I would, if I could, she'd for ever be mine.

Chorus:

But I left my home, in the vale of Glenshee,
There wis naebody there to bid fareweel to me,
I hear the train comin' to be here at nine.
And Ah'll write from the Army that 'I'm doing fine'.

But now as I wonder, my thoughts ever stray –
And my message dear Maggie, near Dalgety Bay,
I envisage you smilin' through eyes blue and true,
And I'm closer to home, old Carnoustie and you.

Chorus: 'But I left my home…' *etc.*
Music, two lines.

My sweet girl back home, is she waitin' for me,
Or is she married now, tae some ither than me?
Way back there then, I was too dumb to see,
My sweetheart had eyes for no other but me.

Chorus: 'So I left my home…' *etc.*
Repeat last line: 'Yes, I'll write…' *etc.*

So if you have a sweetheart, and a penchant to roam,
Be sure that she knows it, before you leave home.
Just tell her you love her, and ask her to wait.
So that when you return, she'll be there at the gate.

Chorus: 'For I left my home…' *etc.*

Tune to be added.

Christmas – Call Time?
A Satire

Composed by Ally Shearer, 27 November 2006.

And there was Christmas...
So... do you remember Christmas, not so long ago,
With fairy lights, the child's delight, 'the family' ordained it
 so?
Do you remember yon time, the sparkle and the glow
Wi' sledge and skate, and the burn in spate, and frolics in
 the snow?

So now they've 'crowned' the crucifix – as an evil thing to
 wear;
And peace between religions, as something else to bear
But I recall 'This England' when no Taliban was there,
With happy pranks on Hampstead Heath, and 'dodgems' at
 the Fair.

Yet Doom and Gloom can't block my mind from the rein-
 deer in my glen,
The Iceland Ponies seen in Wales, nor the Mighty
 Ptarmigan
In their Winter white, and the Raven's flight – as they wing
 forth two by two.
I dream of Snowdrop Valley, and I know that you can too.

Yes, I *do* remember Christmas – here forever, then.
And the women's Christmas 'Hogmanay' in Eire – not for
 men;
But that was Ireland long ago – discovered since, the *hath*
As mountain Nannies teach their young to climb without a
 path.

So, 'Life's Cross to bear, but none to wear' seems the UK
    motto now,
But if we, like Japanese, just simply learn to bow,
Perhaps if Osama and his clan see us humble – this New
    Year,
Then maybe we can live in peace, without perpetual fear
Of bombs and hellish circumstance!
Let Ego Man, the Taliban, pursue his new career.

Away from it all – Aberdeenshire

Cowrin' in the Dark
(Like Hallowe'en)

Composed by Ally Shearer, 31 December 2004; inspired by Briagha, the dog, in the greenhouse, smelling a lump of ginger root.

We were duncin' in the dark,
Doon the Abernethy Park,
Just me and her and ither folk –
Pullin' at me sark –
These Hallowe'ening capers
Are sic a funny lark,
Wid ye 'haud yer weesht'
Frae crowin'… Can't ye hear the *big dog bark*?

(Remember the Devil's got a big black dog.)

Crovie by the Bay

Composed by Ally Shearer, 4 February 2006.
Song, probably 4/4 time, Key F or G.

There's a beauty spot by Crovie,
And a lovely little bay
That should be much more famous –
For I've heard the people say
The fisherfolk so happy –
As they ply their nets by day,
And the clifftops where the people walk,
Look out on Crovie Bay.

Music, last two lines.

There are lots of lovely children
Playing safely on the sand,
It's as if the fine Creator –
Held them in His gentle hand,
No need to go by aeroplane,
To places far away –
Just take a view of Heaven –
In a spot by Crovie Bay.

*Music, whole verse… to: repeat last verse and repeat last two
lines to Fine.*

Croy to Culzean[*]

Composed by Ally Shearer, 27 December 2006, at 12.30 p.m.

Noo – huv' ever ye been tae Bonnie Croy shore?
There's five and twenty caravans, and Ah'm gonne tell ye
    more,
By Maybole's michty yard and Bonnie Maidens too,
Or a sunny Sunday doon at Culzean, where *this* is what
    they do…

Relax and listen while I tell o' the people I met there,
Wi' foreign campers, cars and vans, there was no grass tae
    spare,
From Italy, France and Spain they came, imagine – for the
    day!
They'd never danced this way before, but they're reeling
    anyway.

Noo Strictly Dancing's not the same's we do it here in
    Culzean,
Wi' Brucie's chin and the mighty din – *we'll* dance it in the
    rain,
It's happy entertainment, and naebody had to win,
When Prestwick Ian plays his tunes, ye'll know jist whaur
    ye've 'bin'.

---

[*] Pronounced 'Kulane' and more often in Ayrshire just 'Klaine'.

Yes, I've strolled along this Croy shore, from the Heads of
  Ayr to Culzean,
An' Ah've never seen an eyesore, so Ah'll be there again,
But remember what I told you, when yer feelin' 'roon the
  ben',
Come jyne 'uz' at Culzean Castle, where we're dancin' noo
  – ye ken.

Cruden Bay – Poem

Composed by Ally Shearer, 23 March 2006.

I have left the sweet green fields of Abercrombie,
Where dunes they all sweep down around the bay,
Soft white the sands around my bay of Cruden
Are calling me back home again to stay.

The harbour walks, I gathered in the moonlight,
And Annie Murray's farm seems far away.
'Twas there I whispered fondly to my sweetheart,
'Will you come back again tae Cruden Bay?'

Now I told my friends in Melbourne of my leaving.
In their city of such beauty, I can't stay,
From this land where Scottish pride's abounding,
I now return once more to Cruden Bay.

Now I see again the fulmars winging homeward,
As they swoop to greet the stranger home to stay.
And the corncrake still as lovely as the songbirds.
In my youthful time I spent by Cruden Bay.

Cruden Bay – Song

Composed by Ally Shearer, 23 March 2006.
Tune adapted/based maybe on 'Dingle Bay'.

I have left the soft green hills and homeland,
Where dunes sweep down around the bay,
Soft white sands around my bay of Cruden,
Are calling me back home again to stay.

The harbour walks, I gathered in the moonlight
And Annie Murray's farm seems far away,
It was there I whispered to my sweetheart,
'Will you come back again tae Cruden Bay?'

Now my friends in Melbourne know I'm leaving,
In their city of such beauty, I can't stay,
From this land where Scottish pride's abounding,
I now return once more to Cruden Bay.

I see again the fulmars winging homeward,
As they swoop to greet the stranger home to stay,
And the corncrake sounds as sweet as songbirds.
In youthful times I spent by Cruden Bay.

Dancing Thoughts

Composed by Ally Shearer, Sunday, 5 November 2006, by the cliffs of Dunure.

O'er the water I smile and stare,
Dreamily I know that you are there,
Dog and me, and time to spare,
And croaky cock pheasant as quick as the hare.

You can't see me, as I see you – all demure in your comely
    hue,
Time after time I catch your eye
Far off in the hall, and I wonder why?
Till my heart skips a beat, as you brush by,
Does my ear deceive – did you really sigh?

Then fortune strikes back, as I know she will!
Puts me back on track of another hill!
For that lady luck, with another face –
And the brightest smile in the human race.
Says, 'Dance with me, kind sir – if you can –
And I know you will! – 'Cause you're only a man!'

Dear Santa in Lapland

Composed by Ally Shearer, Saturday, 11 February 2006 (who is a retired 'Lap' dancer).

I shall trouble thee no more,
Nor ramble to your door,
Insult you, or else cause you mi-sery,
Continue to adore you,
And I could not abhor you,
But from you, long forever to be free.

A post-Christmas note from Ally Shearer, aged eight ("Cause I'm all grown up now…").

December Sunshine

Composed by Ally Shearer, 5 December 2006.

December sunshine through the rain,
Makes one feel, it's Spring again,
South-west winds, though cool prevailing,
Foolhardy folk prepare for sailing.
Birds of all kinds sing in trees
Deciduous growth, retain their leaves,
Laid-out apples on their beds,
Gars little children turn their heads.
English apples at their best
Hold your tongue, and hear the rest
Ten years from now as I predict,
The sweetest orange will be picked
Not Californian, or Africa'
But right here in Southern Shangrila.

'Time as norm – six minutes.'

Departure and Arrival

Thursday, 28 October 2004.

Who e'er delivered me this place
O' peaceful hue and flowery grace?
Would that I could clasp the hand
So long departed from this land.

E'er I depart my Heilan' tread
Let no man deem it to be said,
In that place, whaur oor Wallace bled,
Was there no spot to lay this head?

For recognised by friend or foe,
Time has come and I 'must go'...
Back to my land o' hill and glen,
Whaur silver rivers, speak my name.

My dog at heel, o'er mountain crag,
In easy sight o' grouse and stag.
Far from invasion's stoney shore,
Hame at last, to leave no more.

Down the Fiery Glen – Dunure

Composed by Ally Shearer, Monday, 25 December 2006, at 10 a.m.

Christmas with the curlew,
And the big grey gull,
Speed testing brown and furry things,
With Briagh,* have a ball.
The slow droll croak of yesterday,
Simply the big old crow –
I 'wrong-foot' guessed identity,
In the wood, abune the 'heuch'.

Sheep alang the precipice view –
A thoosan' feet below,
Huge boulders meet the Firth o' Clyde,
Some fall, but very few.
The massive midden, Winters well,
Got ready for the Spring,
When corn and barley and all that
Plantation time will bring.

Blessed are we, who share all this,
And blessed are those who don't;
And blessèd be the sun-blest kiss,
That keeps us all from want.

---

* Full Gaelic name – 'Briagha'.

Drumshang Reel

Composed by Ally Shearer, 9 November 2006.

(Opener number idea.)

Well, hullo tae you and you,
Tell me noo, how-do-ye-do,
Too-dle – oodle – oodle – oo,
Tell me, how the 'hell' are you?

The long drive to the short drive

Duncin' Time an' Summer Time

Composed by Ally Shearer, 7 March 2006, poem and song.
Music – Easy reel time.

Noo there's Duncin' Barn and Bothy Yarn and Heilan'
    music too,
Young Andy Cheyne, fae Aiberdeen, mak music wi' his
    mou' –
There's meal and ale and me as well, an' Fergie roarin' fu'
But the funniest thing you've ever seen's, when 'big Tam's
    cast eez shoe'.

Music, two lines.

Noo fine gent Tam Kilpatrick – weel, 'e couldnae dunce at
    a', at a',
An' halfwye thru' the Eightsome Reel, he's stottin' aff the
    wa',
He's soond enuff on tractors, wi' ony mak or kind –
But Tam, and Long John Barleycorn, will leave you all
    behind.

Music, two lines.

Then Ken the Broon – a fairmer's loon – decides to jyne
    the fray,
Since three o'clock at Rocksly Bar – he wisnae suppin'
    'tay',
A wummin' twice the size o' him, did hurl 'im roon and
    roon,
Puir Kenny landed in the Band, and thochtit wis the mune.

Music, two lines.

Noo Seturdi' nite is Duncin' nite – onywhere at all,
Wi' hairst at hame – or corn loft – else doon bi' Hatton
  Hall,
It's Shearer's reel an' anither chiel – is hingin' on tae Tom,
Five mile awa fae sober noo, an' they can do no wrong.

Music, two lines.

Baith lookin' ruff, they've had enuff – an' think it's Louzin'
  Time,
So – tae beat the Band, they tak the stand, for 'Auld Lang
  Syne',
But-the-Band-strikes-up the 'Lancers', as Tam haun's roon
  the mints,
Then heilstergowdy ower the wife-sayin', 'Myn' fa yer-
  bappin', tee-to uppa-ginst.'

Music, two lines.

As baith o' them spreadaggled then – richt across the fleer,
The crowd they clap't an' clap't and clap't – an' then began
  to cheer,
As muckle Tam, the star o' the show – wis kerried oot the
  door.
His Duncie nite wis over, an' you'll see *him* no more.

Music, two lines.

Till Seturdi' nite comes roon again, an' time for 'Take the
  Floor',
When Robert Lovie sings his song, an' Sandy yells for
  more,
Wi' Kenny Mutch – the BBC, an' Robbie Shepherd too,
When 'Problems' all have been removed, we know just
  what to do.

Repeat last line.

Hertford Castle, Herts
Author, right of centre, facing

Dunure Again

Composed by Ally Shearer, 28 December 2004.
(Composed at the time of the tsunami in the Indian Ocean.)

The howlin' winds abune Dunure,
Are music tae my ears.
Wi' problems gone, all banished now,
The world beset by fears.

The batterin' ram, tae face again,
As dog and me set start –
A cosy country glow beside –
The cockles of my heart.

The bothy snug, abune the brae,
Just Briagha dog and me.
We gaze across the rough and glen,
The Firth o' Clyde and sea.

Ten times review old Arran's isle –
But when the lambs are born,
Back here again 'mang kith and kin.
There's no one *here* forlorn.

The railway line – since Beeching time,
A walking, driving lane –
The sight and sound of puffer train,
Will ne'er be seen again.

But take away the manly made –
The stuff of sweat and tears,
The ever-changing scenery,
Now here a million years.

The hailstanes huge that welcome me,
Remind me well of home,
Whaur Heilan' tongues – the rights and wrongs –
Still echo through my bones.

The music and the funny songs,
For me will always last,
While hailstanes – big as Ailsa Craig! –
Now nail me to my past.

I've strolled these Hills o' Carrick,
My spirit soaring free –
As was Easter time, myself and quine
Spied mountains o'er the sea.

The splendours o' Mourne' Mountains,
Again do beckon me,
As Mother, Maggie Simpson,
Regaled me on her knee.

Sweet Boscastle and Cornish lands,
Wi' Devon hills all gone,
Like London Town and Surrey Downs,
Now nowhere to be found.

And now in absent memory
The willow and the stump,
The years of joys and compromise,
Strewth, doth my epiglottis jump!

At last to feel, I am *me* again,
And morn and noontimes thole,
My heartfelt greeting for you is
'*Cued Mile Fàilte*,' after all.

Hath thy will been done?

*(Verse seven: 'Whaur…' refers to Culloden etc. and the Highland
Clearances.)*

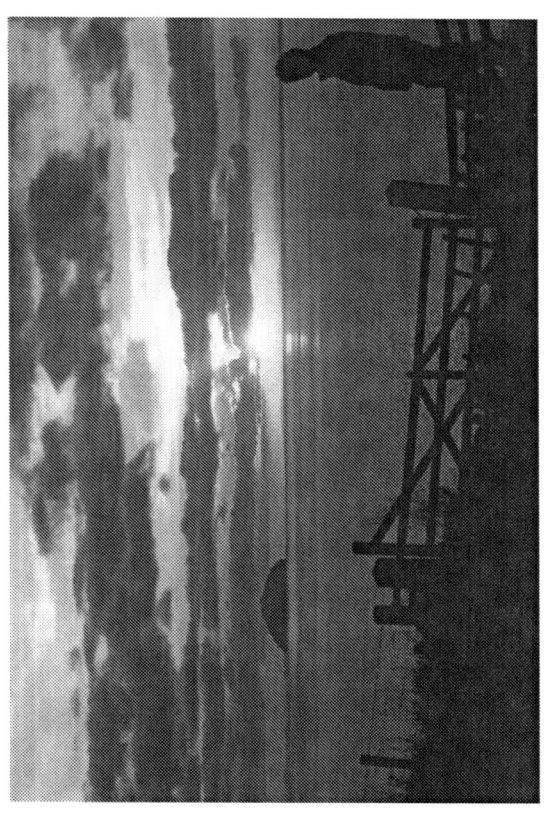

There's Ailsa Craig, All dark like me, And our vanishing sun, Behind the sea…
Like a lady of the lake she beckons me.
The Author at sundown

Easy Girl

Composed by Ally Shearer, 4 July 2005, at 9.30 a.m.

'Easy girl', where e'er you be,
The one you're looking for,
Is plain for you to see,
'Born to remain alone.'
Just simply isn't true,
When the one you're looking for
Is standing next to you.

Repeat last two lines.

Music – to be composed.

Farewell to Ayr

Composed by Ally Shearer – a five-minute poem song – 25 August 2003.

Tune: 'Mary From Dungloe'.

So fare thee well, sweet Ayrshire Toon,
The dearest frien's must part.
The love we knew will aye remain
For ever in my heart.

No sadness now, as apart we go,
From happy days of yore –
But we'll tread oor ways, o' the halcyon days,
As we hae done before.

The Toon o' Ayr will be nae mair,
Not even in my dreams –
Fareweel tae you, auld frien' sae true,
We're parting now, it seems.

Repeat second verse to fine.

NB: Composed for the late Robert S MacGregor of 'Laguna', Ayr, Scotland.

Feathery Snowflakes

4 February 2003.

So white are the hills and the meadows,
White are the streets of the town.
Gently, so gently, are falling
Snowflakes, silently down.

All through the day and the night-time,
Touching without any sound,
Coming from God in their beauty,
Feathery snowflakes down.

A small thing adapted from the memory of childhood.

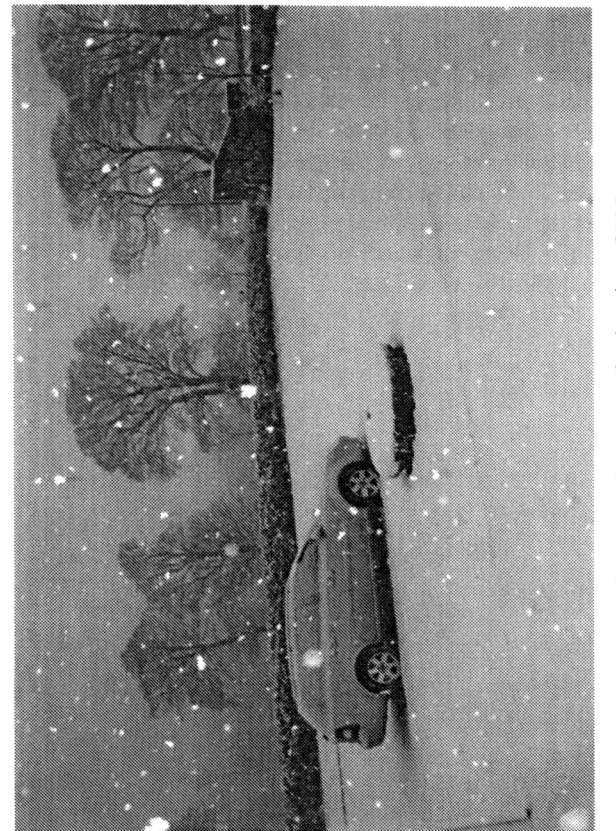

An Arbuthnott Christmas, Aberdeenshire, 2005

Final Bath Time (Welsh Wales)

Composed by Ally Shearer, 29 September 2006.

My time near gone, all spent too soon,
Cannot dwell here – 'October mune' –
September gone, as I must be,
No more to view, *Welsh Wales and sea*,
Roads, back to London, thick and fast –
And tho' sheltered some, from the Winter's blast
I relish fond time, that's nearing now,
When Scotland calls, and I'm there – and how!

Foxgloves and That

Composed by Ally Shearer, 16 November 2006, at 3 a.m.

Inspired by a photo of a tall foxglove amid a pile of fern, on a North Devon hillside – mid-tour, June 2004 – entitled simply Foxgloves and That.

As I start uphill, from my cottage door –
And climb to the sky, till my eyes are sore –
Times I long for my island – 'Real Skye' – I adore,
Where the rains tumble at you, in sudden downpour –
And all is at standstill, yet no one's forlorn:
'It could easily last, till the morra' morn.'

And I recall the joys, of a youth time long past;
'Mid twenty-foot snowdrifts, and the North Sea's blast,
Near the Buchan Ness Lighthouse – and the place I was
    born,
Now the Lizard gales puff by their old foghorn –
Then I hear someone whine, 'Born too soon –
And the climate can baffle – the Man on the Mune!'

After All Huh!

Frannie, Frannie

Recalled by Ally Shearer, 2001/2002.

To a horsey lady on weather and traffic, Radio 2, A.M. Show. She has an appealing giggle and is named Frances Godfrey (must stress, no offence) – and it goes:

Oh, Frannie, Frannie, Frannie,
I wanta' be yer mannie –
Dressed up in my Millenyum Kilt –
The sicht o' me wull mak ye wilt –
Ah'll even trim ma beard fur yoo –
And stuff a pilla' wi' the residue –
Ma Bagpipes huv bin newly tyoond –
And don't they mak a lovely soond!
Ah'll feel sekuwer in certain nollige
That yool be up to steer ma pollige!
Se' fu aboot it, Frannie 'deer' –
Ye ken me weel enuff –
Ah'm a teuch and craggy *Heilander*
No an English pooder-puff!

Och aye, and there's mair…

'Gei's Wimma Fe-Ye'

*Said by my sister Evelyn, at age three years, to her Auntie Lizzie,
meaning: 'Give me, with me, from you' in Babba-talk.*

Composed by Ally Shearer, 24 May 2005.

Put yer glad rags on, an' come for a hike,
You can ride wi' me, on the tail o' ma bike,
Bring yer trousseau on, and yer posh frock too,
Yer goin' to a weddin', and the bride is you.
Weel ye ken Ah'm yer pal, 'cause I bide next door,
I can be lots of fun, and so much more.
So come up close an' hear my plan…
The weddin' is on, and Ah'm best man.
Noo, dinna look glum, or go feelin' blue…
Tho' Ah'm best man, I'm bridegroom too…
So dinna you be late, tae arrive at the gate –
Or Ah'll get tough, although Ah'm only eight!
'Go oan – gei's a kess!'

Girl On a Quad Bike

Composed by Ally Shearer, Saturday, 23 December 2006, at 11 a.m.

Tap o' the hill and standin' still,
Ye'll feel the Southern chill –
Overtook by a girl on a roarin' Quad
Fair bikin' fit tae kill.

A cheery salute, an' a bogey tae boot,
I envy her the thrill –
As she speeds tae feed her animals,
Beyon' the Carrick Hill.

I wonder, wid some younger ones,
Be thinking just like me
Abandon school, boycott the town,
To live, their spirit free.

Guardian Angel

Composed by Ally Shearer, 10 February 2006, at 6.30 a.m.

Lonely Guardian Angel, whoever you may be,
Over and around us,
Everyone and me,
Our endless sky, where clouds roll by,
Our twinkling stars and sun.
The Planets too – just like you –
Since ever time begun.
Where e'er I land, you guide my hand,
And save me when I fall,
Through sweetest joys and earthly noise,
Whatever may befall;
So timely true, life's path renew,
My sacred heart and you.

Halfways Up the Stairs
(The Thoughtful Child)

Composed by Ally Shearer, 30 January 2006.

Halfways up the stairs
She stopped to say her prayers.
And when I asked her, 'Why?'
Cam' her five-year-old reply:
'It's because somebody cares.'

Heilan' Advance tae a Guid New Year

Composed by Ally Shearer, 3 January 2006.

Qs for grub like army time,
Spean's in haun, like yokin' time –
Friendly smiles 'tween loon and quine,
'Show me yours an' I'll show ye mine…'
Sing me a reel – aye, that'll do,
Yin spean plus one, aye, that maks two.
Rattle the gether, and music mou',
Never mind the waltz, just kick up a stew:
Nae time for faults, a hornpipe'll do.
Later on it's a Heilan' Fling –
For 'Auld Lang Syne' ye can hear 'em sing,
Birl 'em and hug 'em, never fear! –
Wir a' prepared for a Guid New Year –
Slanj'e Var!

Hick-Town Girl

Composed by Ally Shearer, 7 July 2005.

Chorus:

Well – she's a Hick-Town Girl – from Louis-ville,
An' Ah've got tuh let yuh know –
She's ma' Hick-Town babe – it's gotta be sayd,
An' I – just love her so.
Ponytail on a buggy-board wail
Stood-up and a shout'n', '*Yo!*'
And that is when I first saw her, a long, long time ago.

Then came last year's Cal-garry rodeow,
Ma eyes they popp't, and ma heart near stopp't,
When I did-see-her go –
'Twas a huge event, and ma heart was sent,
On a buckboard 'circle *yo!*' –
Ma Hick-Town buckboard baby –
Show'd 'em, all the way to go... *yep!*

Chorus repeat; music – band solo.

Well, Ah ask't 'er out – and she gave me a clout!
But her eyes they didn't say '*No*',
I walk'd her back – to my little ol' shack, *Yeh!*
Figured that's the way to go.
'Twas plain to see, she was fancy-free –
An' Ah did love 'er so,
But her love, of course, was the back of a horse –
And a life on the Rodeo.

Repeat last four lines.
Chorus repeat.

Now ma Hick-Town babe's bin gone, Ah'm afraid,
For nigh on a month or so,
'Twas hard to see, but her'n'me
Just had to let it go…
She was Hick-Town buckboard Sally Ann, bound for O-hio,
And my youthful schemes, and boyhood dreams
All vanished in the flow.

Chorus.

She's a Hick-Town babe, it's gotta be sayd
That Ah still love her so –
Ponytail on a buggie stood-up – an' a-shoutin', '*Yo*!'
When Ah saw her a long, long, time ago
She's a Hick-Town girl, an' Ah had to let you know,
Jist had to let her go!

Chorus.

High-Booted Up the Carrick

Composed by Ally Shearer, 23 December 2006, at 12.30 p.m.

There's a dead ewe wi' her gut strewn out,
No need tae staun and stare,
Far worse sights – that I hae seen –
Man – 'tsas if I wisnae there;
For this day I *can* see Arran,
And the Mull of Kintyre forby –
And close at hand is Ailsa Craig, high-reaching for the sky.

A practice 'plane purrs overhead,
A Prestwick jet on high,
And the Carrick Hills now beckon me –
'Come up and take a sigh'.'
Turn my back on the sea's horizon,
Fair level with my eye,
And I understand, why I'm on land –
To hear the Curlew cry –
(*Way up a 'kye* – Scots – childhood – vernacular).

Noo December chill has struck at will –
The neck and kidney too –
But dog and me both fancy-free.
So this is what we do:
We'll tummell doon this grassy hill,
And shelter for a while,
As Lomond and Lochranza's sun,
Does keep us warmer still!
Amen.

Highland Stream

Composed by Ally Shearer, 20 December 2003.

My compliments to virtuoso violinist Gordon Simpson, is the tune 'Heilan' Burn', set in free time, from my Pibroch of that title. These are the lyrics.

There's a lazy Highland Stream,
That meanders through my dreams,
And wanders through my village in the morning –
Sure at noon and night-time too –
It's as close to me as you.
And as welcome as the land where I was born in.

Chorus:

So if you'll come here my queen,
We can meet in Aberdeen,
And we'll ramble through the heather all adorning.
Where the foxgloves stand in bloom,
'Mid the purple and the broom,
Ye'll be welcome in this land where I was born in.

Repeat chorus.

I Have a Friend

Composed by Ally Shearer, 14 November 2006.

I have a friend, a melancholy friend,
I'll say it once again – I've got-a-friend,
Yes! I've gotta loving friend, I'm keeping till the end,
There's no-need-to-pretend, I-have a friend.

Now – I know my little friend,
Can drive me round the bend,
For it's only now'n then! –
I have a friend.

And each time she acts retarded,
It's because she's disregarded,
Till at last I can't deny –
My little friend.

For when she acts all haughty –
And just a teeny-wee-bit-naughty
'Tis then I can't ignore, my little friend –
'Cause if exuberance can show love –
Sure I'm blessed by 'Heav'n' above,
And the world can plainly see – that I've a friend.

There can *be* no greater joy, that she's never been a boy,
And-like-a-meerkat-looking cute she does a beg;
I'm so joyful that we met,
And don't ye know I love her yet –
Especially 'cause-she-doesn't-ever-need to lift 'er leg!

*(L and G, meet my little friend, 'Briagha of Beauly Caledonia', and
I'm Ally S; thank you for having us today; we love you… 'Wuf,
wuf!')*

Briagha of Beauly, Caledonia with her 'Gurry-wurry'; simply 'labradorable'

Imagine Missing Fifty Years!

Composed by Ally Shearer, 6 May 2006.

Cousin dear of childhood days,
Lifelines gone in different ways,
Seems all is blur and haze,
Of countless visions and youth-time craze,

Never a gamble – never a chance,
Seldom a hint of backward glance.
As forward to glory now we go –
Easy the way – steady the flow.

Whatever we find reward will be,
Don't be still to wait and see;
But wend your way to hope and pray,
The Cosmos Guid will come your way.

For Cousin Betty Gillan, Kincorth, Aberdeen.

A celebration of school days with Cousin Betty, Christmas 2005

In Compliment to Jim and Moira McNae of Ayrshire

Composed by Ally Shearer, 24 October 2005, at 3.10 a.m.

Tae Poet Pal and colleague rare,
I met yon day in the Toon o' Ayr,
As darkened cloud did pelt me mair –
Wi'some disdain, and some despair,
As if to say, 'Ye'll Mc-Nae use – jist staunin' there.'

Tae meet in dreich or sunshine state,
In tales o' life and mair relate,
Inside – abune yer gaird'n gate,
Wid seem tae me, no more than fate! –
En route tae man's sweet destiny!

Tae greet and meet in food and wine,
Considered some as mighty fine,
An' sheltered then, frae sna' and frost,
Guid minds in culture, fit tae burst.

Crack the rye – prepare the toast,
Tae a' oor kin, we lo'e the most,
Salute at last, oor 'bonnie host' – Moira,
And 'devil fear the lave o't'!

For here we meet in their fair place,
Nae finer yin could e'er we grace,
Nor view the smile upon your face
When nature's fun beguiled.

We've passed the chance – tae some rehearse.
It's onward now wi' song and verse,
Nae look sae weird need now deride,
We list'en smile, wi' hairts o' pride –
For 'ours is ours' – tae stand or fall –
The world has known us – after all!
The Faither o' invention still,
Is never far frae Carrick Hill.

Inspired by a first meeting and grand dinner evening of a Cued Mile
Fàilte, *at the home of the McNae family in Ayr, Christmas week*
2003.

In Remembrance of 7 July 2005

Composed by Ally Shearer, 7 July 2006, at 10.55 a.m.

Seen on Wednesday, 28 June 2006, at twilight time, whilst watering the flowers. Remembered again, 7 July 2006, early dawn.

I glimpsed a movement, on the ground,
Looked again, and there I found,
In innocence, so soft – profound –
A tiny thing, with eyes *so round*:
She looked at me, and I could see,
She had no fear of me.

The broken-bottomed flowerpot
Is where she chose to be;
I straightened her home, she sat quite still,
And didn't try to flee.
Just looked at me, as if in plea:
'Guid fellow – please let me stay.'

As I became still, I had no will –
The human power had gone
Imagined all my energies, compared to this little one…
Could never quell the power that dwells
In nature such as thee –
Be still thy will, oh little one;
Remain – your spirit free.

This verse committed on the day, nearby eleventh hour,
Preceding noon, a Nation still;
Stand silent without power.
A whole year gone, like the lives *alone* –
Severed by unseen *war*,
More life, by far in the dying star,
And the wee mouse in my bower.

*The above could be called unfinished, and in memory of a discovery in
Ashridge Forest, of the world's smallest mouse; a missing poem which
was jotted and mislaid on an early Spring day in 2005. Hopefully this
will be re-enacted.*

*My ode to the mini above – NB: I'll not be first to spare thee on that
bridle path and* bonne chance, *I won't be last.*

*NB: Reference to the fifty-two lives lost, severed in that cruel hour of
evil.*

In the Dark

Composed by Ally Shearer, 24 November 2006, at 11 a.m.

Middle of the night, as the notion grows,
I tip aroon on my two big toes
A craving for something, tae eat and drink,
Where to look... *quiet!*... and *think*.
No need to look beneath the sink,
Jist brushes and brushes, and soaps that stink.
If the Bairn wakes up – ma' life's on the blink.

So the cupboard's empty, the press is bare
Ah'll search in the fridge, there'll be something there:
Eggs and veg and cheese of the best –
There's blue and green, and I'm goat's cheese blest
But I've spotted the 'Gorgy' – 'Ginzola', that is –
So on with the kettle – listen tae the whizz!
Then sit wi' the oatcakes, pro-active and jam,
And nobody knows how happy I am.
And nobody knows how happy I am.

The Cenotaph, Whitehall

Inveraray Dawn

Composed by Ally Shearer, 20 July 2004.
Inspiration – 'Inveraray in the mornin''.
E Flat, 2/4 time, rocky or steady quickstep; tune adapted.

'Twas a morning in July, I was walking through Inveraray,
When I had a battle cry from the mountains overhead.
I looked up to the sky, saw a Highland sodger laddie,
And he looked at me quite fearlessly and said:

Chorus:

'Will you stand in the Band like a true Highland man
To go and fight the forces all around?
Will you march with MacNeil through Culloden Battle-
field,
When tonight we go to free auld Meldrum town?'

Music, one line.

Said I to that sodger boy, 'Will ye take me to your Captain,
For't would be my pride and joy for to march with you
today,
My young brother fell, of course, and my son at Inveraray
And to the noble Captain I will say…'

Chorus: 'I will stand in the Band…' *etc.*
Tempo to Slow March.

As we marched back from the field, through the shadow of
   the evening
With our banners flying low, to the memory of the dead,
We returned to our homes, but without my sodger laddie,
And I never will forget the words he said.

Chorus: 'Will you stand in the Band...' *etc.*

Ivy Reid

Chorus of my unfinished song in D – recalled from 1950.

Hair of gold, eyes of blue
Lips of cherry wine –
The prettiest girl I ever knew
If we only had the time.

I Want You Here

Started 26 June 2003 – completed 2 April 2004.
Composed by Ally Shearer.
6/8 time; C Major.

I want you here with me right now,
I want you here with me.
Why don't you stay for just awhile,
Why don't you stay? Please come and stay,
Don't go away, stay for a day,
Hear what I say, don't go away.

Whole band in vocal – repeat as decided.

It's a definite John Wright feel.
For a third on a programme piece, or before interval.

Iz It?

Composed by Ally Shearer, Tuesday, 18 November 2003, early a.m. Another for John Wright.

Have we been here before?
Have we travelled through this door,
On our way to nothing more.
Is your heart still feeling sore
And are you lonely?
No more for me and even – you?
Is there nothing left to view,
Are we both so drab and blue –
And both beyond, the blue – so dull and lonely?
Somewhen, somewhere, just – hoping to be true
Both too far away from being homely,
Though *living* once again.

Jist – Oh, Fran!

Another laughable recalled piece from Ally Shearer thus 'entittled'.
Recalled and adapted by Ally Shearer, 13 September 2006.

I can nae langer play yer game,
Ye've kick't me inte touch again,
The verse a' sen' in your *direction*,
Dis not imbue ye with affection,
The rhyme's disyn'd tae mak ye swoon.
An' sen' ye shivers doon yer goon,
Impervious tae a' ma pleas…
Ye jist turn up yer pretty knees!
Unflattered by the wurds I speak –
Lyk watter aff a ducky's beak –
How can you dismiss sic a man –
Anither Yates or butcher's plan –
So… wotabootit, dearest Fran?
I know For You I'm Just The Man –
And if you still resist ma charms –
I'll run away an' eat some worms!

Ken, the Broon

Composed by Ally Shearer, 20 January 2006, at 4.30 a.m.

Oor Kenny Broon was a funny loon,
Kent by a' aroon the toon,
An' tho' his days be numbered soon,
It's considered nothin' drastic,
For very soon, the Melrose loon,
Renowned wid be the world abune
Unnoticed whan alive and weel,
Oor happy soul wis quite a chiel,
His gait, some awkward in the street,
His speech distorted, when we'd speak,
Tho' none for him, wer 'twa scyowed feet',
And smilin' eyes, the folk tae greet,
So spirit bound that life tae cheat,
Oor bonnie Ken was spastic.

Some forty years or so we'd blast,
At times we'd thocht we cursed oor last,
Then sobered-up we'd right again,
He, the spatula, me the pen.
So, mem'ry clear tae start again,
Tae reminisce some now and then –
Army days for some impart,
For ithers, perhaps the broken heart.

Sadness comes, in a' shapes and sizes,
For them that pass receive nae prizes,
Posthumous words sic a waste o' time,
Especially for a pal o' mine,
Drawin' and sculpture were aye his game,
Blessed in spirit's quiet domain,
A dram o' Shanter in 'is haun…

He'd rattle on, as nature can.
Likewise the poet – with his pen,
Mony-times driven 'roon the ben',
In Borders scene or London's storm,
Wir a' the gither – none forlorn – for Divil's scorn.

And as we pass thru' oor wee span,
An' simply dei' the best we can,
Tae save oor lovely planet here,
Will sunshine save, for one more year?
In truth for me there's no Soothsayer,
Wir ilka wan o' us on a prayer –
Wi' 'Hitler-types' an' man's dour greed,
Destroyin' oor blessin's at Hellish speed!

*PS: Oor ain childer, oor ain future. (As Crosby, Stills and Nash once
sang in tune, 'Teach your children well…' Cherish them and rest our
case! – amen to that.)*

Lady Along the Way

Composed by Ally Shearer, Friday, 5 May 2006, at 8.30 p.m.
Song: to my tune 'Piper of Patna' in A Major.

On a summer's day on the fourth of May,
I spied a lady on my way.
She said to me, 'I'm fancy-free,
If you'd consent to marry me.'
So I told her what I have not got,
Attractive – to – a – lady;
I knew I was in a stew,
And didn't know just what to do.

Laffable, Notionable...
Though None 'Speckticulars'

Thursday, 14 October 2004, night-time.

Too much book by the cover: looking to and acting on that first impression (in the digital 'getya, letya' age).

A 'What of' (an ode to the above).

The 'Floers', the leaves, the trees – and all the robes of
    Solomon – that couldn't compare!
An' so to remember: that herein lies a grateful heart maybe
    – the only praise.

A small anecdotal, and thank you to the Sun, which heals our brokenness, and is there yet! And above all and each of our wonderful storms and the clouds which keep our amazing planet alive... after all.

(From my red box music case desk, in some foreign hall.)

Landed in the Dock

Adapted by Ally Shearer, 7 December 2005, at 2 a.m.
A song/poem; tune, trad.; adaptation of 'The Garden where the Praties Grow'.

When first I came to London,
'Twas the year of '49,
The city looked so wonderful,
And the girls looked so divine,
But the Polis were suspicious, and –
I got an awful shock.
They said, 'Yer hair is dreadful –'
And I landed in the dock.

Monologue: They'll nick you for onything – you can get nicked for less even than wrang hair!

Next mornin' down bi' Marlborough Street,
'Mid London's traffic roar,
The paperwork wis busy,
And the telephones did 'burr';
Said the judge, 'I'm goin' to charge you, 'cause –
Ye don't look very clean,
And I'm also going to charge you with
The Offence of Looking Mean!'
Imagine!

Music, two lines.

'Now yer dark red beard and wellie walk,
Will never fit down here,
And stalkin' roon bi' Regent Street,
Won't find you any 'deer',
Yer far removed from tractors –

136

An' machines for trashin' corn,
So ye'll take yer Dartmoor holiday,
An' it starts the morra' morn.'

Now this cell it isn't pretty and it isn't very big,
It's five foot six by four foot, and wid hardly fit a pig,
If I could join the army, at this or ony year,
I'd take my lovely haircut – and –
Just bomb right outa here!

Repeat last two lines.

Lively Thoughts
On Those Less Fortunate

Composed by Ally Shearer, 29 January 2005.

What e'er o' name ye think ye be
Whatever qualifying,
Had ye a mither ninety-three,
And yersel nae fear o' dyin'.

For twa queer feet, we huvnae got
Nor one or them a club,
Fair play tae ye, wha rump and stot
A' roon aboot the 'tub'.

The devil's 'punchbowl' spares nae mair,
Than snob or tinker in its care,
At first they hear then speir nae mair,
Yet yap aroon the lave o't.

If education – as is said –
Steals like infants tae its bed,
Then wakes them wi' a gory head,
Tae curse the like o' thee.

Like boomerangs, the pain returned.
To them wha's erring lips hae burned,
Then doon they whirl, like sycamore seed –
Tae curse nae mair – whaur they lie deid.

The heart of Westminster and Old Scotland Yard

Living Here in London

Composed 19 May 2004.
Key, F Major – solo intro – 3/4 time.
Music and lyrics adapted.

Och, I wish I'd get employment in the land where I was
    born in,
Oh, for I am always dreaming of my own dear native soil,
I can see thon River Gadie, where I was once a laddie,
As she winds and turns, that tiny burn, forever by my door.

Chorus:

But I'm living here in London,
Though my heart is ayewis yearning
For the day I'll be returning
To my own dear native shore.

The village of my childhood days, I see it now through fog
    and haze,
And the grassy banks where I did laze, on there I'll lay no
    more,
And the mountain road I rambled, the crossroads where I
    gambled,
As we pitched and tossed the pennies there, near Wallace's
    old forge.

Chorus: Music to octave up.

Well now, I'm not a scholar, but these lines I'm sure you'll
    follow,
Though a college education I never could afford,
For poverty and hunger, were there when I was younger,
So I thank the Lord these days are gone away for evermore.

Chorus x2.

South Bank, St Paul's, Millennium Bridge, etc. London, UK

Long Before Dawn – The London Heathrow Flite-path Chorus

Composed by Ally Shearer, Saturday, 20 May 2006, at 4 a.m.
(In part somewhat in the near modern idiom.)

Wake – arise, to darkened skies, four a.m. will do,
To kitchen creep, no more to sleep, my medication brew.
Then Burns to read, my own time need,
Till seven o'clock I scent it…
Then up the blind, to happy find, Ric'* Branson's roar and
    hunders more –
Fits me so quiet; contented…
Huge planes so clear – close over here, and sounds I've
    come to love,
Unlike the M-way traffic din, at Hemel up above.

Prevailing winds from Devon way, speed cotton clouds
    above,
'Neath sky of blue, the blatant hue, with memories of all
    kinds of love.
For we can find with peaceful mind – it's easy to forgive;
The fools; like those who've taunted us and told us how to
    live.

Peace be with us all.

(The Orchestration of the Dawn Chorus persists to 8 a.m.)

---

* Ric' – Richard.

Looping the Loop Around 'Oz' and 'Noz' 1997/98

(With reference to the incompleted journal of the time – it must have slipped a busy mind!)

Composed by Ally Shearer, 6 October 2006, night-time.

'Mid the mild December lift-off in the year of '98,
There parted with my one son – fond farewell at the gate.
And many changes happened, since 'Gatport-Airwick' way
    back then,
Like becoming a Granddad four times – Oh *no*! – not again
Kinnell! – Nae wunner puir Jock's skint!

Was my one-off mighty 'nip-off' worth a journalistic note?
I've wished I could relate them, those scribblings – 'wot I
    wrote'
Of meanderings o'er in 'Ozzie' land, not really 'actin' the
    goat'.
A thoosan' copious 'Mem'ries' as I traversed East and West,
But as I recall much overall, my Maori time was best.

From the Bay of Isles to the Tasman Sea – I sailed and
    bussed and trained,
Ten million acres, burned and bare – as their life had all
    been drained,*
And the mighty trains I witnessed, upside down, along the
    track,
Lying on its side – New Zealand's pride – foreign invest-
    ment's cruel lack!

---

* The 'El Nino' time.

I remember well my thinking, Well, ol' England was never
    that way…
But no sooner back in Blighty I was hit in sad dismay;*
However, a journey's hour to Dunedin clean,
Cud-chewin' cows laid in pastures green.

My eyes did smart – 'twas like falling into this Heavenly
    dream,
It had truly rained upon this Biblical scene,
So – from this land's lush green, and hills sun-blasted rock
    and glen,
These halcyon days and Celtic Ways had made me whole
    again.

---

* DVT! First known in UK!

Lover's Promise

Composed by Ally Shearer, 6 February 2006.
Poem/song: Key, B Flat.

You have me for the dearest friend and lover,
You love me for the way I have to go,
When you wonder where love's gone
Like a river-bottom stone,
You should know that you will never be alone.

Perhaps to be continued… Air to be considered.

'Luggage Buggidge'
North, on the High-Tech Train

Composed by Ally Shearer, in Cumbria, Thursday, 21 December 2006, at 2.30 p.m.

Sunshine on the Cumbrian Dykes,
Wi' sheep alang the Howe.
And the Pendolino speeding North,
For the Scotsman's home – and how!

The glistening rivers steady wynd,
As the steel on steel doth ring,
The 'diggidy-da' of the former track,
Is now a bygone thing.

But I've grown used to sitting here,
With a head that's full of song.
Fond gaze on sheep, I nod near sleep,
High-speed we trundle on.

Bound for some equal beauty,
Like the pleasant hills of Ayr,
For Hogmanay I wend my way,
Cued Mile Fàilte, everywhere.

M'aff Noo

Composed in five minutes, 20 July 2004, at 7.15 a.m.
Key F; tune, 'Killybegs'; music adapted.

Chorus:

Well oor time is nearly up, wi've already supped oor cup,
And I'm heading for the Highlands in the morning,
Wi' me wagon and me load, plus me camera and me grog,
It's the bonnie glens o' home I'll be adorning.

In the mountains and the glens, reminiscing now and then,
Of the happy days before when I was yearning;
No need for me to rue, to my country I've been true,
For I've taught them song and dance and so much more.

Chorus:

Though my time be nearly up, and I know I've supped my
    cup,
And I'm heading for the Highlands some fine morning,
Wi' me wagon on the road, I brought home my happy
    load,
And I've roamed again by glen and hill once more.

Chorus repeat; last line repeated again.

Maybe a Lady

Composed 23 March 2004.
B Flat Major.

She's a lady and so maybe she could like a guy like me,
I know somehow, with the know-how, I could plainly let
    her see.

If I tell her how I see her. In my mind's eye – part of me –
Then it's maybe this fine lady could come home to only
    me.

Me and Dogs!

Composed by Ally Shearer, 15 May 2006.
Song.

A big white dog, that barks at flies,
And a smaller black, that wonders why,
From playin' wi' them it's here I lie,
On a 'broken' back beneath the sky.

Briagha of Beauly, Caledonia and Toston, educated Spanish

Midnight on the Hill

Composed by Ally Shearer, 8 January 2005.

At the lights o' Ayr and the 'muckle mair'
Ardrossan, Troon and Largs are there,
All alone I staun and stare –
Am I 'sae weary, fu' o' care'?

No! – For simply I scan the Heads o' Ayr,
Swing roon left, and Arran's there,
The Holy Isle and lighthouse fair,
Am *I* sae weary fu' o' care'?

Noo 'Billy's' awa – in Kiwi Lan'
Biking a hundred miles o' san'
Places I've been and sights I've seen,
Noo *he* – hauds in the 'Big Yin's' haun.

Noo I've seen Seamill and the Hydro fair
The Hilton Grande, the ha'penny stamp flair
Tae judder a man…
Whaur Scotland's Best plays the music deman'
And the ice-cauld plate delivers the flan!

Soon it's high win's gone, and awa tae flee,
The English road for you and me –
Briagha the dog looks oot to sea,
Whaur Ailsa and Girvan will aye be free,
– O' the grockles Manchurian – Devon' scree.

Minnie the Mo-oucha's Birthday

The above word Mo-oucha, *is Hungarian for 'Mother'.*

Composed and performed by Ally Shearer, for Minnie McNae of Polnessan, for her 92nd birthday, 12 April 2006.

Now there's a ge'l called Minnie Mo-oucha,
She's a real-hot coo-chi, coo-cha,
On the dance floor she's a smoocha' – so they say.
An' if you drive down by the wayside,
You'll see Minnie by the fireside,
And for sure you'll have a 'dacent' cuppa-tea,
An' when the tea is over,
You will think you're sweet in clover,
When Minnie's pals come over just to say… 'Ho-hae.'

Chorus:

'Cause it's Minnie Mo-oucha's birthday time today,
And she's just gone twenty-nine, or so they say.
So we're gonna have a ceilidh,
When oor Minnie sings so gaily,
'Cause it's Minnie Mo-oucha's birthday time today –
    'O'yey!'
It's Minnie Mo-oucha's birthday time today! *O-lé! Yeah!*

Minnie McNae of Polnessan, Ayrshire and the Author

Mr Magpie Comes By

Composed by Ally Shearer, 15 December 2006, at 6 a.m.

Mr Magpie came by to visit me, just like the other day,
He doesn't know the joy he brings, when e'er he comes
my way,
He hops and jumps, and walks about – like any other crow,
Gets busy in the guttering with flinging to and fro.

If he could see me standing here – he-would-be-long-
gone-soon.
This very timid gatherer, behaving like a 'loon'.
He digs and flings, like navvies do – stuff landing on the
sill,
He labours on quite happily – there's none impedes his
will.
But-if-he-could-glimpse an eyelash move – his foraging
would cease,
Espied *his* only predator – destroyer of his peace.

So I am glad he comes my way, though now he's out of
sight,
The peck and thrust above my head, I listen with delight,
And I know that he'll return again, departed from his hen.
I've viewed his kind of arrogance, from since I don't know
when.
And now as climate changes loom, it's grand he comes so
near,
And I feel I'd like to say to him, 'Fond Christmas and New
Year.'
I study and I contemplate – try to relax my head,
But then I spot 'His Majesty' – and watch him go instead.
C'est la vie!

My Arran Isle, O!
(Poem)

Composed by Ally Shearer, 7 January 2005 – Dunure, 5 p.m.

I've a friendly neebor living here,
Keeps me happy thru' the year,
Wi' her in my view, I have nothing to fear,
She's a lady so fine my sweet, Arran Isle, O!

I see resplendent lying there,
Her sleeping Warrior, shoulders square,
And I know why he sleeps so fine,
In the arms of yon sweet neebor mine.

I've walked along Broadway, seen nothing so grand,
Travelled so widely through every land
Wander back to some well-beloved spot in your dreams,
You'll-find nothing so fair, as my Arran Isle Queen.

How green was my valley, that I left behind,
Lochranza, Goatfell, my sweet mountain climb,
Brave ferries bring people, from near and afar,
To view sights as fine, as the great Lochnagar.

Fare thee well my guid neebor, away I must go,
And trudge o'er the highways and hills high and low;
But I'll soon wander back to the place that I know,
And you, my fond neebor, sweet Arran Isle, O!

A daily sight of Holy Isle and Arran
But different every time
Never twice the same – pure magic!

My Arran Isle, O!
(Song)

Composed by Ally Shearer, 8 January 2005.
Key, B Flat to F.

I've a friendly wee neebor, living quite near.
She keeps me so happy, thru' all of the year,
When I view her serene, I have nothing to fear,
She's a lady so fine, my sweet Arran Isle, O!

Music, one line.

I can see all resplendent, so still lying there,
Her old sleeping warrior, with shoulders so square,
The reason he sleeps so restful in soul –
Is he lies in the arms of my Arran Isle, O!

Music, and that last line repeated vocally.

I have walked along Broadway, seen nothing so grand
Travelled widely and freely in every land.
Wander back to some well-beloved spot in your dreams,
You'll find nothing fairer than my Arran Isle queen.

Music, last line repeat vocally.

How green was Glen Rosa, that I left behind,
Lochranza, Goatfell, my sweet mountain climb,
Brave ferries bring people from near and afar,
To view sights as fine, as my dear island star,

Music, and last line repeated.

Fare thee weel, my good neebor away, I must go,
An trudge o'er the highways and hills high and low.
But I'll wander back to the place that I know,
And you, my fond neebor, sweet Arran Isle, O!

Repeat music and last line vocal.

Oh dearie me! Lochranza, Isle of Arran

My Cottage on the Borderline of Mauchline Town and Ayr

Composed by Ally Shearer, 23 January 2006, at 5 a.m.
A song in a rocky quickstep or foxtrot; Key, F or G Major.

Is there any point in dreaming, when you're not really
   there?
Is there any point in scheming still, when they don't really
   care?
The ones now gone away so long, and the homely place is
   bare,
In my cottage on the borderline of Mauchline town and
   Ayr.

Music, one line.

If you believe that love is here, for ever and a day,
I know a different story, to you I'm bound to say,
When day is done and they're all gone, the laughter and the
   play,
We stand alone and wondering, will they return some day?

Music, one line.

The little dreams, the 'girlie' screams, the giggles and the
   fun,
That lifts our hearts, reminding us, we're better off than
   some,
I know I'd trade a million things, tho' now I never can,
Just to hold those tiny hands again, and feel a happy man.

Repeat last two lines.
Two chords – repeat verse one; raise key or modulate; music,
two lines, with vocal to finish.

My Lovely Rose of Ayr

Composed 14 March 2004.
F Major, 3/4 time.
Lyric and tune adapted by Ally Shearer.
Arranged by Ally Shearer and Flora McCrae.

Chorus:

My lovely rose of Ayr, you're the sweetest girl I know.
The Queen of all the roses that in the garden grows,
You are the sunshine of my life, so beautiful and fair,
And I will always love you, my lovely rose of Ayr.

As I walk along the river bank beneath an azure sky,
I listen to the little birds, sing-songs for you and I,
With lonesome happy memories of all the people there,
My heart remains with yesterday and my lovely rose of
    Ayr.

Chorus.

And now to say farewell to you is more that I can bear.
And travel on my journeying without you being there;
So soon to part will break my heart, as if I didn't care,
But I will always love you, my lovely rose of Ayr.

Chorus x2.

By any other name

My Ode to 'Pear-Shaped' Villa

For Sue and Ken Plaw (Sook and Blaw – Two Fine Pipers)

Wisbech, Cambs, 3 August 2003, by Ally Shearer.

My wife has died, I should have cried.
But the house is falling down.
The donkey sighed and the horse has shied,
So I'm headin' back for town.

I'm on the run, the floods have come,
It's just that time of year.
But I haven't got a problem –
What could be left to fear?

The concrete's 'mixt' – the chimney's 'fixt' –
What else is there to do?
Sit and think, but never blink,
I might just think of you.

All said and done, I've had some fun.
Now I must take my leave.
No going back, along that track –
No time left to grieve.

So if there's else that's left to do,
And I have left this patch,
I'll take my load and hit the road.
No other plots to hatch.
Just wind my way, no more to say –
I've got a bus to catch!

My September London Sunrise

Composed by Ally Shearer, 7 September 2006, at 4 a.m.

Awake to starling chatter, all windows open far,
The azure sky replacing, my Planetarium star;
I feel the muffled converse, nearby my window sill,
And the morning sun has now begun, to wrap around me
    still,
For Autumn's dewy coolness has not imbued us yet.
Though multi-changes can take place, before our sun has
    set,
I feel each day in its passing way, is like a life full blown –
From rise and shine, to sundown time – just one day older
    grown?

But first enjoy the starlings' muffled chatter on the breast,
From feathered friends more peaceful, in *their pattern* have
    digressed.
Though closely one by one, no fidget in them yet.
Nor to face the rising sun, just increase – 'tête-à-tête' –
Unfolding show, completely free, on chimney pots ablaze,
No rush to stumble from my cot – as if in drunken haze,
For golden sun from Thamesmead – now glinting through
    my glaze,
I'll waddle t'ard ablution scene, much like other days.

Huge iron birds of Branson, Brit' Airways and the rest,
I wonder how they do it, as they're into Heathrow pressed,
Great bodies gleaming gold-like, as they thunder through
my heaven,
No need to whisper this time, as it's now gone well past
seven;
But a noisy peace surrounds me here, of this I've long been
sure,
Contentment lies beneath these skies, though some would
think me poor.

My Sometimes Song

Parody/adaptation by Ally Shearer, 13 November 2002, at 5.15 a.m. Rocky quickstep.

Chorus:

Some broken dreams never end,
Some country roads never bend,
On memories of you I'll depend,
And my love for you will never die.

Some things in life we just cannot mend.
And some things we've found, with more than a friend,
Some things we'd love again and again,
Like the nearness and dearness of you.

Chorus.

Sometimes I feel you, so close to me,
And then realise, this never could be,
But I'm blessed each day when in dreams I see
You standing right here next to me.

Chorus – band in solo, including harmonica.

Each day there are times, when I hear you call,
Times when I climb so high, again just to fall,
Tho' I seem to smile, as I climb the wall,
Till I see that down here, there's nothing left at all.

Chorus.

So here where I land, is where I will be.
Here where I stand, with you close to me,
And as you hold my hand, the whole world can see,
There's more here than dreams – just for me.

Chorus.
Repeat last line to Fine.

Never Twice the Same
(Marriage Happens)

Composed by Ally Shearer, 19 June 2005.

Och I'm sad, if I do upset you…
And I'm sad I ever met you…
You're the one – that made my life a misery,
At times I could have told you,
I'd very gladly gone and sold you –
But alas dear girl, they've banished slavery.
But then if I'd never owned you –
I never could have known you
And I'd never have enjoyed sweet mystery.

Music, one line; or repeat last three lines, vocal with band as required.

Och I'm really glad I met you,
And I never would upset you,
If you hadn't gone and spilt my cup of tea.
But you never need to flee,
For there's no one in this life but you and me,
Though I canna say I'm sorry –
There's no need for you to worry –
For there's no one in this life but you for me.

Repeat last two lines to Fine.
Probably a song for e.g. Music Hall.

Ode to Love

31 July 2003, by Ally Shearer.
Song.
(Slowly – A ballad in the John Wright style); Key, F.

So, were it not for this love of you,
Who knows where I would be?
Banished by some agent hand
To lands beyond the sea,
To live through different nightmares,
So far from you and me.

Music – line/s to suit.

Chorus:

The happy accidentals – like meeting on the stairs,
Those tiny instrumentals, so far from people's glares.
The music of some heartbeats, not meant for you and me.
More solo than a duo – in lands beyond the sea.

Band in one line.

Our accidents of nature – that meeting was for sure,
The Mona Lisa in your smile – the limbo I endure.
The drumming of a lonely heart, was surely meant to be.
Far, far beyond the complexity of things like you and me.

Chorus: 'The happy accidentals…'

Your long blonde hair and easy way, so plain for all to see.
Still thrums away for ever, in some land beyond the sea.
More duo than this solo, it still holds them all entranced.
To see again before them, the gem of music dance.

Repeat line, to –
Chorus: 'The happy accidentals…'
Play twice – to fade.

Not even thinking of the 'Moo-cow' Restaurant, Notting Hill

'So what now brown cow?'

View of the Bay of Ayr from the high Carrick

O Lovely Toon o' Ayr

Composed by Ally Shearer, 17 February 2005.
F Major; tune adapted.

O lovely toon o' Ayr,
As everybody knows,
The sweetest of them all by far,
As through your river flows,
The fairest o' them a' aroon,
You've been our pride and joy,
And still you're happy to remain,
Since Rabbie wis a boy.

Chorus:

My lovely toon o' Ayr, my love,
Affection for you grows,
You're queen of all the county towns,
As everybody knows.
You've been the sunshine of my life,
Since first I cam' to you.
And come the day when we must part,
'Twill break my heart in two.

Repeat last four lines of chorus to Fine.

On Early London Dental Destruction

Composed by Ally Shearer, 3 January 2006.

Saved alone by my Heilan' skin,
Unlike my teeth, no longer in,
Cassidy's drill for profit main,
Ruined my 'chaw' for profit's gain.

Our Kirkconnel Maid

Composed 2 November 2004.
Song, C Major (G or D).
Lyrics original; air adapted; slow 4/4 or 3/4 time.

There's a graveyard in Kirkconnel,
There's a cottage in the Glen,
Where once there lived a maiden,
Who inspired the hearts of men.
She was handsome, fair and hearty
And as graceful as the dawn.
The whole world loved that maiden –
Pure and lovely Maureen Bond.

I recall the day she left us.
For her fortune and her fame,
As I watched the big ship sailing,
I could not apportion blame;
Though my heart was wrought asunder,
And my love for her was true,
As I lingered by the harbour
I just knew not what to do.

Music, two lines.

Time and years passed by, till one day
Came a letter o'er the main,
And I could not keep from wondering,
Would my love return again?
With our tiny children growing,
Will she ever come again?
With the flowers all sweetly blooming,
With our darling home again.

Spoken, not sung:

On a day I well remember,
Came a bell-ring at the door.
And 'twas then I saw my darling,
As she never looked before.

Raise the key.

For her look was as a stranger,
And her cheeks were pale and wan,
And at once I knew the danger,
Of my losing Maureen Bond.
In the Churchyard in Kirkconnel
Near my cottage in the Glen,
Lies the angel of my lifetime,
Who inspired the hearts of men.
She was handsome, fair and hearty,
And as gentle as the dawn.
And the whole world loved that maiden,
Sweetheart, darling Maureen Bond.

Music only last two lines to finish.

Our Time

On a train at noon – (six minutes) Our Time.
Composed by Ally Shearer, 28 March 2006.

Well! Now that time is racing by
Imagine – dream – as here I lie
Of a place called 'Heaven' by and by –
Beyond that clear blue Lifeless Sky
What then, this bliss called Life? I sigh.

If hardship equals paradise –
Though to convince me otherwise, they try;
For *your* God and mine, is you and I,
As together we see, our spirits fly.

Nature Abounds
Till the Vile Do Their Rounds

Composed by Ally Shearer, 10 May 2005.

Dogs 'n' trees, an' bumblebees,
More dogs than deer.
And sadly, plenty else to fear –
At Frithsden Beeches playground.

December 11, 2005
No wildebeest, nor buffalo,
No alligators too,
But still attracts two-legged rats,
As from posh lairs they spew –
They tear from town to town,
All threatening people's lives
And revving through the forestry –
Their 'plaything' four-wheel drives.

For chumps like these their purpose,
Is whirling round and round,
Full headlights on – plough on and on –
With blaring 'foghorn' sound,
In dead of night with 'speed-of-light',
They rout the creatures out,
The frightened hinds, by mindless minds –
Just know not where to run.
Some perish 'neath the churning wheels –
While vandals have their fun.

No need to bag – 'our wondrous stag',
The carer of his herd,
Who'd yield no quarter in fair joust,
Directing from his crag.
His troupe would gar 'them' four-wheels spin,
With bellies in the air
And deep within that sinners' bin,
Screams, 'God, this isn't fair!'
So – how to teach the foolish few,
Who deem to have their way:
It's blessed 'Mother Nature' who has the final say.
And we who wait and don't berate
As to the manner born,
Remembering how our parents were,
Stay silent – with our scorn.

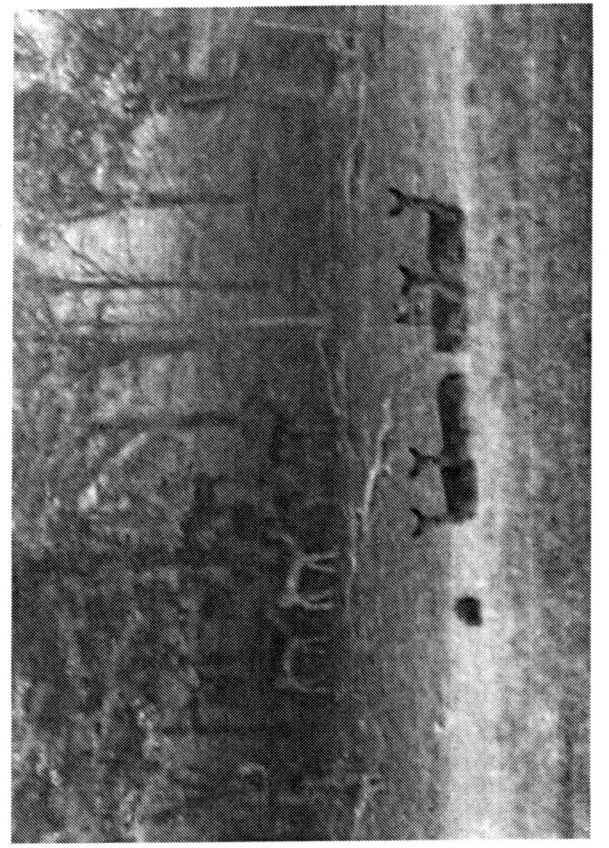

Nature abounds to be sure – Ashridge Forest, Herts

Postcard to Pal Jim in Ayrshire

Composed by Ally Shearer, September 2006.

Jim Lad. Ah'm staunin' here, ma back tae the wa'…
A'-tapa' this hill, wearin' naethin' at a',
Whaur a mountain's a hill an' a mole's-heap an' a' –
Yin thing Ah'll admit t'ye, the wither's gey braw!
Aye to be sure! It's a bit like Dunure.

Ravines and Sheep Fields Around Drumshang

Composed by Ally Shearer, 19 April 2006 – Drumshang fields.

The sheep-clad fields and Beeching track,
Sniffy dog keeps looking back,
Triangles in the bluebell wood,
And daffs all nodding like they should.
Rhododendron in the woodland glade,
Blooming brightly in the shade,
'Pinky' primrose pushing fast,
Heeding not the rushing traffic past.
The croaking pheasant vents his song.
Sloe's open arms to the buzzing throng,
What else to need for Spirit free,
Than the budding of the hawthorn tree.
The stymied well, no welcome now,
For Summer hand that mops the brow.

These notes were jotted during memories of childhood days among Highland ways, during one of my countless peaceful walks and thinking times around Dunure, below the Carrick Hills of Ayr, and from Croy to Craig Tara, and the Heads of Ayr. So far from the rushing-maddening crowds, of the towns and cities of England and London, in particular; with their soul-destroying non-'freeways' in between. The contented soul and mind of a happy heart – 500 miles from anywhere *– without travelling upward to skyward. No queues here – only cues – to the next lovely scene from nature; showing us how infinitesimal we are, and reminding us of our mortality.*

No thoughts of mint sauce – just the 'being there'

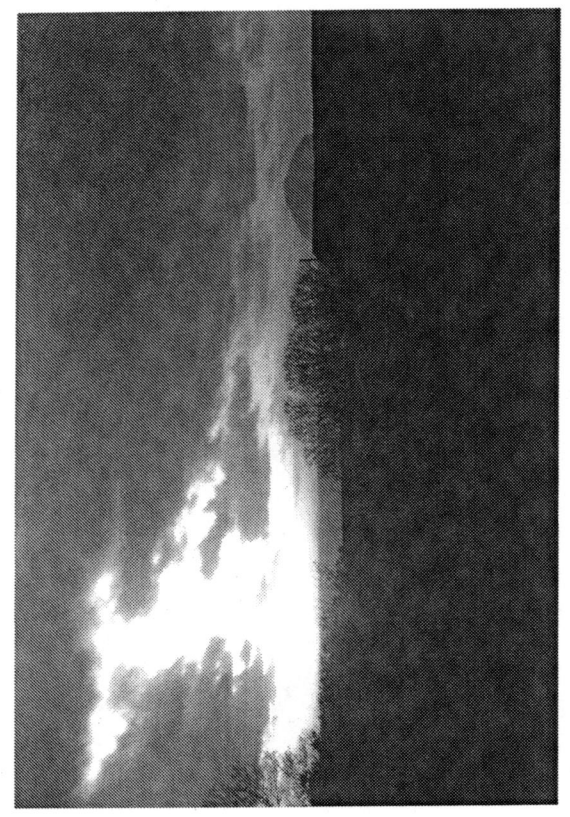

Ailsa Craig in late December sunshine
Firth of Clyde – from our rear window
Observe Scotland's silhouette in the sunshiney sky

Reminiscence in December Sunshine

Composed by Ally Shearer, 7 December 2005, at 1 p.m.
Tune, trad.; adaptation of 'The Garden where the Praties Grow'.

Noo I've been searchin' roon and roon.
For words I canna find,
The tunes they're stuck inside ma head.
And stood the test o' time.
For I hae left my Highland home,
Some fortune for tae find,
And the tunes keep furlin' roon and roon,
The corners of my mind.

So I made masel' a list or two,
O' the ones I miss the most,
Sometimes I'm jiggin' roon aboot,
The kitchen and the toast,
And ither times at drivin' roon,
When Ah'm completely lost,
And then in foreign lands you'll hear,
Sae far across the sea,
That ilka Johnnie Foreigner
Looks doon and pities me.

It's then they see that puir auld me's
Not really roon the bend
Fur I can gar 'em lauch and dance,
Like happy Heilan' men!
(Och aye… nae bother.)
So the nearly loon, fae Heilan' toon,
Is headin' home again.
Aye, the nearly loon fae Heilan' toon,
Is headin' home again.

RIP *the Muntjac*

Composed Thursday, 7 October 2004.

Wuz it yoo wot 'kilt' the muntjac?
Ah said, 'No, it wisnae me...
Fur Ah even luv the foxis – it's pretty plain to see –
And I couldnae kill a muntjac
Fur I luv 'im runnin' free...
So, wha'ever 'kilt' the muntjac,
Don't ye look again at me... *if* you don't mind!'

Ony Herts, Beds and Bucks folk here? – 3 CTYS Radio?

Robins – 'Don't Migrate – for the Italian Dinner Plate!'

Composed by Ally Shearer, 1 October 2005, at 5.25 p.m.

There's a hungry breeze on the top o' the trees,
At times I can hear the robin sneeze,
Puir wee soul, he's brought to his knees –
But escaped the nets o' Italy!

Rock It, Babe
(A Song)

Composed by Ally Shearer, 27 January 2006, at 6 a.m.

Well now, you gonna show it to me,
Ah'm gonna show it to you,
So-now-you-hang around, and you'll see,
Ah'll hang around it for you.
Come now you, you're gonna rock-it to me,
Ah'm gonna rock-it to you,
Come here now and see,
Ah'm gonna show *you* what to do.

Well now, you show it to me
Ah'm gonna show it to you,
So now you hang around and you'll see,
Ah'll hang around it for you,
Come now, you, you're gonna rock-it to me,
Ah'm gonna rock-it for you.
We'll be rockin' for free,
When we go rockin' for two.

Ad-lib as necessary to continue or Fine.

(Think Van Morrison style.)
Idea for the music established!

Roon the Dog's Leg, Farm Lane – tae the Royal Tournament's Farewell
(Ode to my Fulham, West London, abode, circa '59)

Composed by Ally Shearer, 2 December 2006, at midnight (begun Autumn 2005).

Down Farm Lane by the Buddleia,
And the roses gone to seed,
Where Rowans outshine in majesty
Convolvulus, bindweed:
Where drains are blocked and no one talked.
But joggers, jog for speed
As overhead the Concorde,
Wid waken up the deid.

This place that I returned to,
For nigh on twenty years,
Has seen the ring of changes,
Through blood and sweat and tears.
To dwell back then in mem'ry –
'Worth-living' – fit – to – last,
In sunny climes and loving times –
Would nail one to the past!

Big Tom up on the policeman bike,
Bent-pipe between his teeth,
Full twenty stone – muscle and bone
Who never caught a thief.
Tom was our 'village Bobby',
And lived among us then,
The friendly 'mass deterrent' –
And the kindliest of men.

To be born in the year of *Legends* –
On 'Stadium' it is seen,
Earl's – Court – Report; 'twixt fashion shows.
On high, I saw the Queen –
'Salute' my Hundred Pipers[*] –
As 'Her' 'Gordon'[**] took the Quaich,
The Sovereign Major scaled the heights –
We all had kept the faith.

Not much tae show, for a working life,
For countryside and Queen;
Not much to show of 'Married Wife',
Now nowhere to be seen.
Though bairns three returned to me,
After – nothing – said – or – done
And I am the one contented;
It's like, 'Thy Will Be Done'.

---

[*] Yin Hunder Pipers, of all ranks and regiments – a large percentage 'Has-beens',
with respect.
[**] Pipe Major Gordon Webster, 1st Batt'n Scots Guards.

Sandy Bodie – Buchan Loon
(Nae Fae Only Ither Toon)

(Watch out for the anticlimax before the end!)
Composed by Ally Shearer, 21 March 2006.

Noo everyone loved Sandy – since the day he went to
    school,
There was six foot two of Sandy, and he wis naebody's
    fool.
Poor Sandy didn't learn much – and he never used to rave,
But dived deep doon the whirlpool – the lassie for to save.

Now to every school the bully – likewise some clever fools,
A multitude o' characters, and them that spurn the rules:
The big lads oft-times quieter – content to play the game,
Geo' Harper, he was one o' them – 'But watch oot jist the
    same!'

The smaller fry, as time wint by, aye yumpin' up and doon,
Desperate for eye-level, and tryin' tae rin the toon,
But oor Sandy was a gentle soul, and rin nae-body doon,
Instead he'd meet you wi' his grin – tae brighten up the
    'mune',
That Smile as wide as the countryside – when he'd ask you
    for the time,
Then off he'd shamble once again – tae see what he could
    find.

Harmless as the day is lang, wis Sandy Senior's son,
Wi' a' would vouch for Sandy, for he could do no wrong,
But when he met the bully, that night on the edge of town,
Puir terror struck on Sandy's luck – as he felled yon bully
    down.

For years he'd poked and taunted at poor Sandy – blushed
and shy,
Till that fateful night, in the bright mune-lite, when Sandy
at last let fly,
Noo the bully's Dad, already mad, was trackin' Sandy
down,
Bi' the playgroon' gate, he lay in wait – but the Dominie
came around.
Noo the bully's heid wis stuck in the gate – till the fire bri-
gade could call.
And happy Sandy's gentle life was lovely after all...

For a gentler soul than Sandy ne'er breathed beneath these
skies.
Nor fonder heart of life itself – in terra firma lies,
And if you were to find the spot, in a glade not far from
here –
The finest floers are *Sandy's*, *all seasons* of the year.

*Monologue: Sandy loved picking and presenting wild flower
posies and sharing his observations of plants, shrubs and buds
in the varying stages of bloom, along with all insects and wild-
life. One was blessed in his company.*

Scotland Again

Composed by Ally Shearer, Friday, 27 October 2006.

Shut the night out, put the light out
Hear the loud wind whistling in the trees;
Feeling jaded, and I've said it,
Some journeys bring me to my knees
Not the M-way, or the airway,
Given up now, as life's extremes;
Let the train, take the heavy strain,
Branson's 'Pendolino' in the main;
I'm heading homeward, yet again –
Tho' feeling jaded – yet upgraded,
Back once more in my land of dreams.

The Highland Piper by Balquhidder, Rob Roy's family resting place
A sight and sound for the stranger's eye and ear at any time

Sleepless in Fulham

(A tipsy-eyed observational philosophy, 12.23 a.m.)
Composed by Ally Shearer, 24 July 2006.

Ye come tae me wi' yer comely hue
And try my weakness thru' and thru'
But I who's lived as long as you,
Knows how tae deal with the bold untrue.

You're quiet and homely-way approach,
Seems like no one could e'er reproach.
But takes the noble heart to know,
For Highland ways ordain it so.

A grace, much higher than is thine
The quest they beg in 'Auld Lang Syne',
The honour that – which Burns has told
Twa hunder years does yet unfold.

For one who takes the short cut now
Is one whose fate is sealed somehow,
Let others see the damage done,
As tragedy befalls everyone.

Quote: 'That much to learn, that much to know!'

So I Said to the Horse – 'What's wi' the Long Face?'

Composed by Ally Shearer, 24 November 2006, at 11.10 a.m.

Och – a miserable face can go no place
It's the worst damned thing, in the human race;
So Ah'm gettin' anither, just in case
I get fed up or feel disgraced;
'So face – you're my fortune,'
Ah'll-buy-a-spare-one… How?
Salvatori the 'Ice Creams' – selling them now
Huh! So I'm two-faced now, burra won't be long,
Feel six foot high, and Ah'll Zing 'Ma Zong'.
But here's the truth, tae close this space,
I'd-much-raither-be-the-owner o' the Funniest Face;
For if Laughter is Health and Wealth, *I'm sure*
You'll be my pal 'cos I'll never be puir.

Last two lines repeated as:

Yes, if Laughter *be* Health and Wealth, I'm sure
You'll be my pal 'cos I'll never be puir.

Someone Else's Problem

Composed by Ally Shearer, 16 October 2005, during October 'Springtime' at Ard Choille.

We'll never see our spirit rise –
Or where our humble body lies –
As everyone who lives and dies –
We're someone else's problem!

Whether we 'peg' in some foreign land,
Downed by some unruly foe,
Unwelcome on Iraqi sand,
It's someone else's problem!
Like *'When we go'* – *always is* – someone else's problem!

Somerset Stone

A poem written on Monday, 28 July 2003, by Ally Shearer.

By yon river Frome and a Mendip Hill, a beaker of tea and
    none to spill.
The sun near high and hot as hell, seven o'clock and a tale
    to tell.

On a 'wooden' pumpkin, I face the sun.
As for all good folk, the day begun.
Hear the hum of the traffic's boom,
I sit and think near Rossetti and Sassoon.

'Twas here on this climb, on the fine Clay Hill,
Millennium things are gleaming still.
New oaks and rowans do tickle my face,
While others cut short, for lack of space –
Was it the God who granted such a grace?

Mushrooms abound 'aroon' my feet.
Bunches galorum, and oh so neat.
Nettles are stinging my arms and legs,
But the mushrooms do gleam like pullet eggs.

The invisible groan – as the goods trains pass.
Laden with rock of Millennium past –
This toon in the valley now complete? –
So fast – and another to build, while materials last.

My gentle dog's ramble enjoys her run,
Soon it's the young one's giggle and fun,
The dew on the grass could wash 'yer' face! –
Soon I'll depart – this blessed place.

This sojourn all over, and history too,
I must meander for pastures new,
This England so fine – this beautiful land,
Six decades now free, from that foreign hand,
I too will be free, in the past of my time.
But 'noo' – cheerio – I 'hae' mountains to climb.

By Frome, Somerset
See on the horizon the first of the Mendip Hills

Stay By Me

Lyrics by Ally Shearer, 10 May 2005.
For the tune 'Margaret and Gordon Leslie's Waltz', by Rob McCombie.

If you stay by me, my love,
Our world will be as one.
For I've travelled far, my love,
From where I first began,
If you stay by me, my love.
We'll see horizons new,
And time will not be long, love,
When I can stay by you.

Chorus:

I have longed these years gone by,
Whenever time allowed,
Days and nights beneath the sky,
I always did avow,
You're here within my reach,
I cannot leave you now,
You stay by me, my love;
Our world will be as one.

Repeat first verse.

St Stephen's Day – Tsunami
26 December 2004

Composed by Ally Shearer, 18 January 2005, at 3.40 a.m.

Since well before all time began,
For every woman and her man,
And Nature scuppered, as Nature can –
Through all eternity.
To try and change a scheme so grand,
Is way beyond the 'right of man',
And must as mighty rivers ran…
With pure perplexity.

No hope for those who think they can –
Do better, than old Nature's plan –
To save herself as planets can –
Their sole and only destiny.
And surely those who watch and wait
Like the shorthorn bull at the high-barred gate,
The roar doth come, that spells the fate,
For all who know – yet stand and wait.

So, for the likes of you and I
Planets split – volcanics fly,
And drive their innards to the sky,
What's there for humans to deny?
Though beasts and birds all know the 'why'
For they are part of Nature's try –
To save herself – for by and by.

Summer 1976, 'Victorian London'

Rediscovered, Sunday, 19 March 2006.
Sometime in the dark and early hours of the coldest Spring (2006) in
memory for thirty years – I dreamed a dream.

Flash memories of London streets,
And paltry costermonger treats,
Dried up neep-heids, sold as greens,
'Sonny Bussey' vents his spleen,
But-ye-widna'-see-*that*! – North o' Aiberdeen,
What do they know – poor city folk –
O' them veggie cheaters, and they're no joke!

Sunshine Dog

Composed by Ally Shearer, 23 January 2005.

Here with dog in Gadebridge Park,
Better in sunshine than in the dark,
For then I can only hear the bark,
And none of the joy of her romp and spark.

Sweet 'Syringa'

Composed by Ally Shearer, 28 June 2005.

*Rocky tempo, D Major (Medium Jive); tune – 'Wabash Cannon-
ball'-type US tune, tho' not same as; adapted – from memory.*

Intro. Chorus:

How I love you sweet Syringa
As the orange blossom tree –
I-do swear my sweet Syringa,
I could love no one but thee.

Band in banjo and box.

Oh the orange blossom special,
Is a thing so sweet to see,
And the orange blossom special,
Like the rain in sweet Dundee,
The both of them remind me –
Of the ways it used to be,
When the orange blossom special,
Was the time for you and me.

Chorus.

How I love you sweet Syringa
As the orange blossom tree –
I-do swear my sweet Syringa,
I could love no one but thee.

*Solo blues harmonica with hush-'plonky' backing from banjo
and box.*

When the time comes sweet Syringa
You'll consent to marry me,
We'll go roamin' in the gloamin'
To our home in sweet Dundee,
And the song that we'll be singin',
Is the sweet Syringa tree.
For I love you sweet Syringa,
Y'r the only gel for me…

Chorus and repeat.
(Maybe up key or 1/2 i.e. semitone.)
No break – straight into chorus and repeats, last line e.g. to
fade!

Tell Me Darlin'

Composed by Ally Shearer.
Another 'Wright idea', 6 February 2003.
With Expression, i.e. 12/8 'Freetime' feel, like pibroch.

Please tell me darlin', whenever you're there,
I feel so free, like the birds in the air,
And when I first saw you, did my heart take a turn?
Was it simply for me that life had begun?

The bad times and good times all blend into one,
So why, tell me why then, can't we be as one?
Are we both in heaven, am I on the run?
Will you tell me darlin' – will we be as one?

Possible band music line.

Time is all gone now, wasted and done,
Will you tell me darlin' – when all's said and done?
Are we going somewhere – or just having fun?
Do we meet the angels, and then be as one?
Tell me my beauty will we be as one?

Is our time all gone now – the whole of it done?
Do please tell me, darlin', have we just begun?
Or are we all over, with nowhere to run,
Shall we meet the angels and then be as one?

Repeat last two lines, from 'are we all over…'.
John Wright style/technique: Band in – box in front – music,
i.e. some near individual line/pieces, to piano in front/ditto/to
mandolin in front – fading to hush! – to vocal solo in.

(A mixed-up lover's questioning lament).

Tesco's Hill

Composed by Ally Shearer, 1 April 2005, on early dog walk.

There was Briagha and me on Tesco's hill,
And wee Jenny Wren, I could hear her trill,
As I trod along, she just sat there still,
And singing her song just for me...

But the skirl o' *Ard Choille* is ca'in' me back,
From the bracken and gorse of this 'concrete track'.
Back to the days o' my river and glen,
The purridge and stovies – and happy again,
Since I've been awa, since the Lord knows when –
Frae the 'Foo'r ye dein?' and 'Ah'm a' richt, ye ken.'

Noo some do travel to broaden the mind,
But me I imagined a fortune to find,
And if fortune be life – weel never you mind –
For when I have landed, contented I'll be
Settin' my snares by the Don and the Dee.

That Isn't the Question – This *Is!*

Saturday, 14 August 2004, at 6.50 p.m.
A song inspired by John Wright.

So where have we come from, to land just here?
From a place far away where we knew no fear,
From a time so sublime in our days so young.
When well waters were clear – no harm had been done.

So where on our sphere d'we imagine we are,
On this globe of such beauty, that once was a star?
When 'moments' ago – it was buckets to well –
And the now of tomorrow – what's there to tell?

Och! 'there's little worth mention' – after all's said and
    done –
A remark you'll hear often, all under the sun;
But if that's your 'deserve' through the tears and the fears,
And the doors you kept slamming between your two
    ears…

Then what of perfection – when you dreamt you'd arrived,
Through struggle and strife, though you'd barely survived:
Did ever your thoughts in their fancy take flight
On the long lonesome road or the darkest of nights?

Well! – Were you like me, while finding your place?
And the sweet serendipity put smiles on your face –
Ignoring the conflict – you strode travelling on –
Just followed your chin – kept marching along.

PS: Making sure in your mind perhaps – that you'd finally arrived.

That Was Long Ago

Composed Thursday, 27 January 2005; Rocky/ Lively/ Jive/ Quick-step; Key, C/D.

You and I were young,
You and I were young,
Nothing had gone wrong,
But *that* was long ago. *(Repeat line.)*

Our song has all been sung,
For that was long ago *(Repeat line.)*
Our heads are not so strong,
For that was long ago *(Repeat line.)*

And we have done our song,
For that was long ago,
Yes we have done our song,
For that was long ago.

Band solo.

The past has all been lost,
For that was long ago,
The future, it was won,
And that was long ago.

And since our time was free,
When we went on the run,
Fine time for you and me
Our life had just begun. *(Repeat last two lines.)*

Our 'spirits' on the run,
There still is plenty time,
Enough for you and me,
Enough for you and me.

Repeat first part from beginning to 'long ago'; ad-lib to fade.

The Bluebells Do Survive
But Mony Floers Gone

Composed by Ally Shearer, 9 May 2005.

A hen alang the road
Like a thristle 'mang the corn
Is noo a rare sight indeed.
Like the yowes in the knowes
(It's a' people hae'en rows).
We look, but canna hear at a'
The skylark sing.

The Cockney's Smurfday

Composed by Ally Shearer, 12 July 2006.

Inspired by the 'Londoner's Birthday' and with reverent memory of the 'Mighty Bow Bells' laid flat on waste ground (1959 and 60s) opposite the site of the Dickensian-era Newgate Prison and Paupers' House.

Tune TBA. Readers should 'imagine' a song about Lowry's 'Matchstick Men and Matchstick Cats and Dogs'.

Cor blimey, it's me Birfday!
Maybe *now* I'll have my say –
'Oo's smurfday is it anyway?
Sing, 'Happy Hip Hooray!'

So the Birfday feed again has come my way,
There's really no escape for me today,
I'll stuff my face and tum
While sitting on my bum,
'Cause it's Grandpa's Happy Birthday time today.

Well I had a mighty feed,
Developed quite a need
Though there wasnae ony speed – or so they say,
Tho' youse don't really care,
Not one morsel left to spare,
And surely can't you see, the problem now with me.
Is, how to get me 'bum' up of this chair! – (Jim McNair!)

And repeat ad-lib when sung.

The Covert Extrovert

Composed by Ally Shearer, 12 May 2006.
Tune based on 'All For Me Grog'? (Dubliners.)

A-laffin' and a-jokin', drinkin', and a-smokin',
Till the lovely Summer daylite did come in,
No need to have a double.
To keep me oot o' trouble,
Aye happy through the music and the din.

Music, whole verse.

We wifey inside waitin', as her man is oot creatin',
Far better than indoors committin' sin!
After all was said and done – she is the only one,
'Tho' he's oot there havin' fun',
Jist waitin' for the future to begin.

The Dancing Song

Lyrics by Ally Shearer, 25 June 2005.
To the Strathspey tune for John and Margaret Bellis by Rob
McCombie ('Trudgin' Roon Aboot').

We are trudgin' a' aroon the place,
And on fae toon to toon,
Just enjoying a' the space,
And a-jiggin' roon and roon,
We hae torn oot and worn oot.
Near a' oor dancin' sheen,
Thumbed a hunder mile or so,
Frae the Broch tae Aiberdeen.

Och t'wasna' funny,
When the weather wasna' fine
And Peterheid tae Aiberdeen's
A loup for loon and quine.
We'd dance and grab the chance,
Wherever we may be –
Bi Hatton or the Brig O'Don,
Or doon by sweet Dundee.

We huv danced aroon Dunedin,
Perth and Melbourne City too,
Roon aboot the world o' Dance,
And the music kept us true,
Well the Spirit o' the music.
Brings the Dance to me and you,
And the trudgin' roon and roon and roon's
The thing you've got to do.

Repeat from '…the Spirit'.

In dancing mode with Ian Muir Scottish Dance Band, Crieff Hydro, June 2006
Author in foreground, right. Facing camera: Mrs Flora MacGregor née McCrae of Kilmarnock

The Dancing Trees

*A poem/song composed by Ally Shearer, Saturday, 15 July 2006, at
2 a.m.*

*Monologue re. the gentle breeze and the moving trees, especially
the Acacia in full bloom:*

The big tree's dancin' in the garden
If ye tell me it's the wind, I beg your pardon!
Huge arms all sway around
Bodies rooted to the ground,
The big tree's dancin' in the garden.

No mune is shining yet,
But I can see the silhouette,
So violent and profound below the garden,
Very soon they're holding hands,
'Ring-a-Rosie' on the land,
It's a happy little band down in the garden.

Music, two lines.

Now the mune is climbin' high,
Stars are dancin' in the sky,
Will it all end suddenly and without warnin'?
I for one will not forget
Why I'm stickin' with it yet,
Come the daylight will it all end in the mornin'?

Music, two lines.
Repeat verse three starting with the word 'Will'.

The Dawning of a Day
(With Venus, Gulls and Jumbos)

Composed by Ally Shearer, 19 November 2004, at 6.15 a.m.

As from my humble bed I laze,
And through my window – Venus gaze – alone with
    mystery.
The azure sky grows brighter still
Beyond my leaning window sill –
While whispering jumbos glide at will –
Their silenced power all o'er me.

As out of the night red, green and white
Come silent huge and flashing lights
To signify that all is right
Another day has dawned
Towards our destiny.

What e'er may be our plan from here,
Have we got more to fear than fear?
For all our hearts hold truly dear
Close by or o'er the sea,
From skelping youngsters or parents' faults
To heinous happenings end result –
It must be held, God only knows,
Our plan was laid already;

Let them who think without remorse –
Imagined, solitary recourse
Of life with value less than them –
Their greatness be the power to stem –
The miracle of all.
Our tears and trembling hearts disdain –
Will Kingdom ever come again?
Through prayer to ever heal the pain.

Returned to view the Southern sky –
But there before my very eyes –
All Venus and her sisters gone –
And left me standing all alone.
Yet still the khaki planes sweep by –
A glint of sunshine warms them
Companions now, the croaking crow doth moan –
I friendly feel towards him.

The Dream

Composed by Ally Shearer: verse one, 28 August 2005, at 10.20 a.m.; completed 28 February 2006.

Oh I dreamt, last night –
'Twas heav'n I was in
With a million flutes there, to welcome me in.
There were so many smiles, I'd go there again
To leave far behind, the world we are in.

I've had dreams before,
A hundred or more.
And there isn't a doubt I'll have many more,
But of daydreams and nite dreams,
There's one thing I'm sure –
It's only in nite dreams –
We find something truer.

Have you got a 'Dreamtime', like some people do?
Of 'Abos' and Druids, I know quite a few,
When most 'normal' people, to sleep will resign,
Others keep vigil – six hours after nine.
For what are they waiting,
There's no one will tell –
But wait for their 'Dreamtime'
As if in a spell.

So stay with your dreams
Perchance they'll come true,
Whether you live them, is all up to you,
They say, 'Follow the fellow – that follows the dream' –
But to follow your own
Is far better it seems.

The Dream Awakes

Composed by Ally Shearer, 12 July 2006.
To Jane and Flora – the Killie 'Twins'.
Tune adapted and variation of it, from an old traditional Celtic Air –
i.e. 'Shannow River'.

Last night I had a pleasant dream,
I woke up with a smile,
I dreamt that I was back again,
On dear old Arran Isle,
I viewed afar the Criffel Hill,
Where flowers wildly grow,
And I saw the grave o' Rabbie Burns,
Where the old Nith River flows.

'Twas then I saw old Killie Town,
With her happy people there,
Where memories stir the sleeping heart,
That beats so full of care.
But the Ayrshire town where I would be
That nestles by the sea.
And where her river gently flows,
Is home sweet home to me.

Music, first two lines of verse two and singer repeats last five
lines from 'Where memories…' etc.

The River Nith, Dumfries

The Fields Abune Dunure
('A Prood Dog')

Composed by Ally Shearer, 28 December 2003.

Noo rinnin' up a river –
Is a dirty dog's delight.
Easier-by-far than swimmin' –
Just to get it right.
An' if *you* be Labradorable –
Like me – and I'm a dog –
You'll love to roam and ramble,
When the geese are in the bog!

Twa birds, licht broon wi' necks so white –
Started at my feet;
In speedy flight, ne'er oot o' sight –
The swoop o' bendy beak –
Were I so fleet, along the street –
I'd hae twa smokie paws –
Ah, but then I'd hae them in my power –
Inside my lock-tight jaws!

As soon's I saw them –
If I could draw them –
I'd do so in duration.
So you could see them wild and free.
All in the new plantation,
An' Arran's Isle I view and smile.
As sun and cloud surprise
The snaw-capped heads aroon' Goatfell –
Go meeting wi' the skies.

For Briagha of Beauly Caledonia.

'Dirty dogs' no more – delight, yes

The Flatlands of Suffolk

Composed 28 September 2004.

With the hedgerows all gone, and the loss of birds' song,
Lonesome people so all alone,
Now heard pleading in plentiful song,
'Wind farms are wrong,
Wind farms are wrong.'

Beautiful Suffolk with trees and vales,
And streams in abundance, and Tudor tales,
All kinds of farming went right off the rails,
When 'chilblains and toothache' brought their smiles to
    wails.

Suffolk, like Norfolk, with fields of maize,
And sweetcorn grows, while sheep do graze,
Kind folk recovered and women provide,
For comfort stops with animal rides.

When all can gain spirit,
Who know nothing more,
Of the hellish upheaval, that came to these doors.
Of the hellish upheaval, that came to these doors.

The Floribunda Waltz

Composed by Ally Shearer, 14 March 2004.
Key, F Major; 3/4 time.

Now listen here and I will tell of music fine and free,
Where once I lived by Highland time, 'mid heather hills
and trees,
We'd waltz and sing, we'd dance and fling, until the
morning sun.
Then head for home, no more to roam, before the day
begun.

Chorus:

We'd dance and sing and Highland fling, our troubles all
set free.
The world was ours, for hours and hours, my floribunda
flower and me.

The Gamekeeper's Daughter
(Tae Catch a Badger – Heilan' Hen Food Thief!)

Composed by Ally Shearer, 21 April 2003.

The gamekeeper's daughter, ye'd think he woud've taught
   her
That the root'n-toot'n and shoot'n
Just ain't for gals like she,
And if ye wanti' catch a badger,
Ye jist canna be a cadger,
Withoot a gun or snares or owt –
Just you wait and see!

So I showed her, 'cause I knowed her
By the white upon his forehead,
It's easy for to trap 'im,
Jist standin' still ye see – wi' patience in the dark.
White hanky 'like a bat'
Ye kin trap 'im, just like that,
As he's creepin' roon the hen-hoose,
Lift yer cudgel, let it flee.

The title of the above 'epistle' – 'To Catch a Badger' – just think o'
catching a bat. (Tell the story of bat catching with a hanky.)

The Granite Glen for Me

My ode to New Lanark, on leavin' sic a place; o' a man's ingenuity, havin' spent the hours and visited yet anither pairt o' Scottish History and Heritage – April 2002.

Composed by Ally Shearer, at New Lanark, Easter Monday, 1 April 2002.

And the michty Clyde,
Sae deep and wide,
A-tumblin' roch and free.
Some hunder horses white as snaw
Here racin', just for me.
Aye – as lightnin' white a' thru the nite,
Since surged MacGregor's name,
Frae there to here, this blessed year,
I hae come hame again.

Abune twa thoosan' feet o' hill,
The roughneck craws, aye braggin' still,
For 'oors and 'oors I hear 'em shout –
'Hey! Come see – the daffs are out!'
The barkin' dog, the leppin trout,
The 'flutter-by', the bee,
The ripplin' streams o' England gone,
This granite glen for me.

Guid mornin' Scotland!
But alas it's cheerio the noo.

NB: Moments before composing the above poem, I had hurried blindly straight into a large broom cupboard (poem idea surging in my head) while being urged to vacate the YHA room! Much to my personal comic shock and horror and to the delight of the young cleaning ladies… Grrr! C'est la vie!

New Lanark – a truly amazing achievement

The Grumpkin

Poetry in the modern 'eejit', perhaps.
Composed by Ally Shearer, 16 October 2005.

So in some corner all forlorn,
The one who once had dreams – like all of us
And talent some to spare
But now – to see him crouching there,
In character all laid bare.

I make my case – for human grace
As lived – and ends in storm.

For Terence Puskas ('OCSI') – Hungary's first genius footballer.

A rare testimonial to a rare sporting character, RIP.

The Hame o' Willy Starr

Composed by Ally Shearer, 23 July 2002.

In-the-vale o' lovely Stirlingshire,
A Scottish genius lies…
In a gaird'n there aside the kirk,
Beneath the Scottish skies.

He faced them in his gifted youth,
So able in his prime… against the footlights' dazzle.
He'd play till well past time: and then
When life o' night's all past, gave way to morning's sheen,
The Willy Starr accordion was nowhere to be seen.

The time was running short for Will –
His tunes all fading fast.
The genius o' the early days,
Was over now at last.
His Polkas and the 'Jacqueline' – a memory soon to be;
The magic dancing fingers – we ne'er again shall see.

The cancer o' the vertebrae – a terror to be sure…
But the everlasting music is the thing that will endure.
And so dear friend on Croy's sweet hill…
Fond memory lingers still – of sweet strathspeys and jigs and
Reels… set feet on tapping trill.

Your like we'll never see again, for ever and a day,
From Grampian to Edmonton, we're glad you passed this
    way,
Tae sing and mak the fairies dance – I've oft-times heard
    them say;
Ye'd laugh and joke – when e'er ye spoke,
And taught us how to play.

Yours Aye,
Ally C Shearer, New Pitsligo, Aberdeenshire.

*NB: Will Starr – worldwide artiste, stage, screen and radio, who used
to cheer all backstage, prior to his bounding on stage where he electrified
his audience and he'd say, 'Have ye heard the mavis singing?'*
Quote by kind permission of Will's two sisters, Rosie and Theresa.

Will Starr, 1959 – the Author's mentor

The Happy Eighties?

Composed by Ally Shearer, 14 February 2005.

It's four a.m. and no one to share,
Just me and the old dog Floss
But nobody there, with frost in the air,
So what's there for me now tae cross?
And what's there to care for –
But dreams of a love long and lost?

Into the burn of the dry Devon sun,
All Celtic feelings – tarnished and gone –
But what if the new magic life's just begun,
There yet may be time to have fun.

Read ye now then, of a time long gone
And think of some joys never known,
And of not knowing why it never did shine,
The feelings sublime, in some far distant time,
Where smoking and drinking were never to 'rhyme'.

When the true loving friendships seem fewer and fewer,
As we longed for a love that for ever endures.

NB: Some people's lives.

The Happy 'He and She' Hound

Composed by Ally Shearer, 5 January 2006.

Noo the 'he-hound' and the 'she-hound' set oot on a roam
 one night,
O'er Highland Glens and mountain Bens, till stars were
 shining bright.
An' oor Rabbie wrote o' twa great dogs, baith wunners sic
 as these.
They to'd return wi' daylight, twa stamachs for to please.

Oor twa great tykes, ca'd Bill and Sykes, were ayewis
 makin' fun,
Baith rakin' roon the fairm toon, when ilka day begun,
Their daily fare was chasing hare, aroon each rugged glen.
An' then by nightfall's suppertime, tae snooze and dream
 again.

Then as the new day does unfold, twa brithers free once
 more.
From patience true personified, agin' that 'open' door,
Their need tae ramble far from home, frae mornin' noon
 till night,
Shows bitter sceptic anywhere, our genius Burns was right.

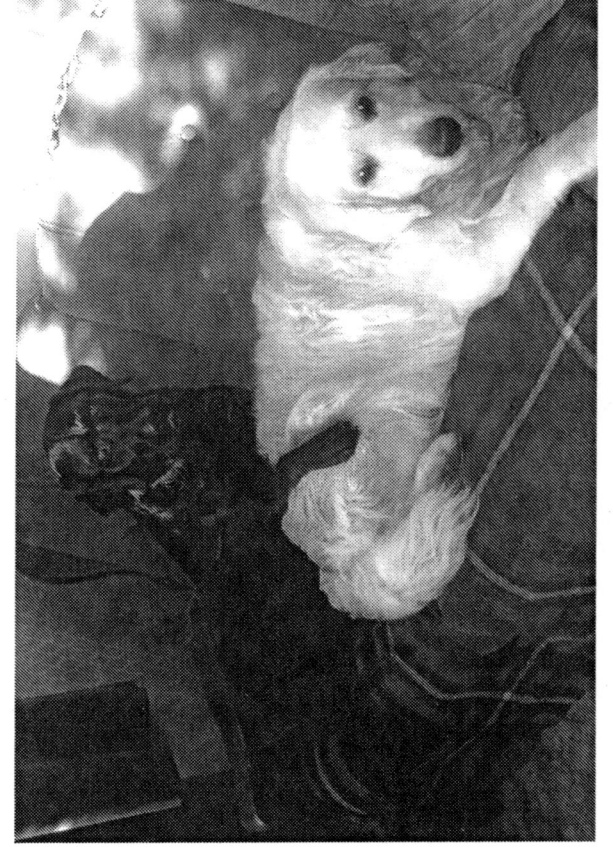

'Come on, get up, I want to'
Briagha goading Toston, the escapee from Madrid – so happy here

The Have-Been Men and the 'Lady'

Composed by Ally Shearer, begun before awake, a.m., 19 March 2003.

An ode – to the Aspirers of Life! i.e. including those who speak of 'The Blondes', both the 'dumb' and the not so!

I sit and trim as the sand runs through,
Trimming the wick as I think of you;
The flame – now even – to Gold from Blue,
And I ponder still, of the things you do.

Here in the quietness I think of you,
Alone and still by the fire-glow's hue,
Amid such peace – what else to do? –
But contemplate and dream of you.

With your comely grace, and look so pure,
You fooled them all – like no one truer;
But as they who learn – get fewer and fewer –
Time favours those – who got Bluer and Bluer.

The good times collected, the souvenirs too –
With your hair of gold and your eyes of blue.
There's we who know, there's none of it true –
As we sit and smile – and – think – of – you.

The Highland Heart in Me

Composed by Ally Shearer in the quiet midnite hour, 10 November 2005.

'No Savagery In Hearts Banished by Necessity' and so saved as in 'The Ode to Love' below.

Not, alas, for all tastes, this sentimental interlude; perhaps only to be shared with the truly brave in Highland Heart – that may never have been fully reconciled. (The savage loves his native shore.)

Were it not for this love of you,
Who knows where I would be?
Banished by some agent hand,
To lands beyond the sea,
To live through different nightmares,
Far, far from 'you and me',
In spirit never free.

To only dream of heather glens,
The lapwing and the trees,
The lonely heart, so ever green.
An' pollen from the breeze.
Dear land, where you lie waiting,
Beyond the churning sea.
Pray do one thing, my heart to zing,
Like honeysuckle bee.

Just save for aye my Heilan' burn,
And bonnie rowan tree,
The Corrie Glen, where mountain men.
With hearts now winging free
Once more the Capercaillie
And big black 'grousey' hen,
Do spar and bow, in private war,

Their 'rutting' time again,
Then stop and stare, wi' time to spare –
As my silent stalking tries:
Magnificence in Osprey – all nesting in the skies.

This throbbing heart, no more to part,
From love so great as thee,
Your iron-eerie water's
Sweet music sets me free.
For I've come home, with you to roam,
'Mang heather hills and deer,
A million miles from anywhere,
Ten million miles from fear.

On the West Highland Road from Gairloch
Guarding his hind – seen in the background

The Hillsides of Scotland

Song, composed by Ally Shearer, 29 March 2006.
My tune 'Rahene River', Key, F Major; 3/4 time.

The Hillsides o' Scotland, they travel so high
Sometimes you would feel that they'd reach to the sky,
Then from old Ben MacDhui and the Cuillins of Skye,
You would think it was Heaven you were driving by.

Chorus:

With their white misty cap on and coatie forby,
The stags with their hinds and the rivers run by,
You can view the red sunset on mountain and glen,
When the Hillsides of Scotland lie sleeping again.

Music solo.

With a lifetime to ramble, a heart filled with pride,
The sweetheart you found down by Loch Sheilin side,
With each new day a-dawning and turn of the tide,
Close cometh the hour of your own mountain side.

Chorus, repeat.
Music solo.

Now the long journey over, and time to recall,
Australia, New Zealand, New Guinea – Nepal,
The high towers, the ghettos, the icebergs that fall.
We soon realise we could not see it all.

*Chorus, repeat – then repeat verse one and chorus again, repeat
last line to Fine.*

A view between Grantown-on-Spey and Tomintoul

The Isle of Love

Composed by Ally Shearer, 23 March 2006.
Song, D Major, 3/4 time; tune adapted from a traditional melody.

Oh – my Mother heard me answering the telephone one
day;
That youthful time when love was blind, I knew not what
to say,
I calmly hushed your love away, it seemed the thing to do,
But I've rued the day you went away and wonder – how
are you?

Music, one line.

I do wonder dear through all the year if we should meet
anew,
Would you consent to marry me? Imagine me and you,
Your sunshine smile and calm beguile, to warm me thru'
and thru',
And a hunder mile, I'd walk the isle of love to be with you.

Music, two lines.

Now Australia's sunny shores they seem a million miles
away,
Can I survive so far from you? – It's hard for me to stay,
I think I'll pack my bags and go, just leave here right away,
And bid farewell to this living hell, for heaven far away.

*Up key E Flat or G – vocal in – last two lines verse three and
repeat last line to Fine.*

NB: *Love is the island.*

The London Flite

Composed by Ally Shearer, Wednesday, 3 November 2004.

Now I depart this London town.
None first to turn this way around,
For many men, more famous found,
Their time had come to flee.
From Highgate's Hill by Marx's glance,
Like Krakatoa's lively stance,
Or Hampstead's Heath, where gypsies dance,
They've turned and seen it gone.

To search alone for fairer space,
Camaraderie ourselves to grace,
To laugh and talk with honest face,
Is hard-earned destiny.
So away then from this 'crowdy' place,
Rejoin perhaps the human race?
Back to where I still belong.
And listen to the thrush's song.

Thus were I not to make my move,
Uproot from this unholy groove.
Or lie earth't up like ony sheep,
Be gratefu' for a Lowland sleep,
The 'oft-sprung' heritage all used up,
Of some real-life love, I took my sup,
The quaich then, for my final cup
My spirit then to free – *Slanj'e Var*!
Where e'er *ye* lie… I'm done!

The Morning A-rose

A short 'Poem' in the Modern – as well as Medieval – idiom!
Composed by Ally Shearer, Wednesday, 8 June 2005.

So off I shall drift away –
Into the future and *not* the past –
Ambling by, and never too fast –
Down Farm Lane – I meander again…
Under the cloud, into the rain…
No worries nor fears – *no pain*! my dears,
Feeling quite *guid* – fur-a-man-o'-my-years,
And morning comes – late Spring, warm and calm…
Then I am reminded – *not* of yesterday,
For out there like a *Monet* – in the 'Poppy Field'
'*She*' – pauses; serene, pale cupped hand, supportingly,
She savours the sheer beauty of life in a single rose.
And fondly I remember 'Yes! I'm *alive*! – all the time'.

An English rose

The One Road

Adapted by Ally Shearer, 1 March 2005.
G Major; 2/4 time.

Chorus:

We're on the one road, taking the long road.
We're on the road to God knows where…
We're on the one road, maybe the wrong road,
But we're the gether, now who cares.
North-men, South-men, comrades all –
Aren't we the best when our backs are to the wall?
We're on the one road, singing along…
And so we can't go wrong.

Maybe we've had our troubles now and then,
But we always make it up again,
Aren't we all brothers anyhow?
Let's join hands and sing together now.

Chorus: 'We're on the one road…' *etc.*

The Passage-less Time

Composed by Ally Shearer, 23 February 2006, in SW6; a p.m. poem, very late.

(A brief thought on some o' mankind's callousness.)

It came to pass, these times foregone –
And some survive withoot a clone;
A Planet changed from this one now –
And slowly spun, in search of snow.
Will the Sun still burn the dewy morn?
Who'll educate the newly born?
When Mums and Dads – a thing long past,
And wedded bliss nailed to the mast.

Would we, all born so long before –
Still yearn for the thing we now adore?
Will greed and avarice aye remain
With 'Can't Afford' oor ain domain –
And, 'Welcome Friends' – be real again?

When oil and gas – no longer there –
Hands, endless time to wait and stare –
Will schemes and dreams, perchance fulfil?
Will folk still work against their will? – at ending time,
As every hill, and valley lie 'neath oceans deep –
And our Lifeless Earth – doth for ever sleep?

The Road to 'Muchty
and My Memories of Jimmy Shand

Composed 11 February 2005.

When first I went to 'Muchty
'Twas the year of '88,
Wi' eleven days of rain
And rivers a' in spate.
I was glad I'd been in 'Stakis' place,
Wi' Tam and Happy Jim,
Their music was as pure –
As the suit that Jim was in.

Till cam' the day eleven,
I had no plan at all
A look at Capercaillie,
An' I wasnae there at all.
The Bank o' Allan Water,
So peaceful and so still.
To the sound of distant bagpipes,
The heart swelled tae the thrill.

I paused there for a little while
Wi' precious little aim.
Then I saw the kilties comin'
For the Brig' o' Allan games;
I'd never seen such colour,
In a warming August sun,
And I yearned to be among them,
Where we a' could be as one.

But mind made up, I'd saddled up
For Auchtermuchty Fair.
But for tug o' war, the egg and spoon,
And marathon I was spare,
Yet I landed o'er bi' Braeside,
Somebody for to meet,
Though first I didnae see him,
Doon by his gairden seat.

Three times and more, I trod the path
That led me to his door –
I felt a fear and trembling –
Like I'd never known before.
I couldnae knock, or ring or talk,
'Twas better I should leave –
But final time, on downward path,
I truly did perceive.

'Hullo,' said I, near walking by,
My legendary host;
Before me – true born genius,
Just readin' his *Sunday Post*.
Into the park beside his place
This giant of music strolled,
His friendly Scottish welcome,
Meant the story must be told –

– Of how my camera failed tae work,
So I handed it to Jim,
And the Guardian Angel stopped all time.
As I stood next to him…
The simple photo taken I treasure for all time,
Wi' me in 'ad finitum',
That happiness is mine.

Now when the living legend,
You visit for a day
Does quietly in the handshake –
Just look at you and say
'Bring oot yer box, and we'll hae a tune –'
The mind's in disarray!
But you fumble oot the Ranco
And wonder – *Can you play?*

The tune 'My Home' seems far off now,
The things he said that day,
'We're a' jist ord'nary folk' –
Tae me did humbly say.
Each breath and pearl of wisdom,
Like notes he used to play –
What wasn't said, spoke volumes,
Of the man I met that way.

In September, year 2003, I travelled back again,
Clackmannanshire, and Waverley – doon Devon's bonnie
    Glen;
The sky was blue, the sun shone too,
No words of thanks could say –
How hearts were all a-tremble –
As we went for 'Muchty way.

To meet our need,
We downed our feed,
In the Café Tannochbrae,
Where played a wind-up 'Master's Voice',
That softly seemed to say –
'Thank ye a' for comin'
Ye're a' welcome here the day,
Were it not for you, it's a' sae true
Nay need for me to play.'

No more to do but join the queue,
Of the thousands there to see
Unveiling for a mighty man,
Now part of history.
Full six-foot bronze looks over all,
Sets feet a-tappin' free
A' o'er the world, we waltzed and burled.
The man'll never dei'.

So now as time is passing and
Wi' each mon tak oor turn,
We'll stroll along tae Jimmy's plot
An' back bi 'Muchty's burn.
Time to think o' brilliant lads,
Wha carry on and play –
All thankful, just like Jimmy Shand,
Who simply used to say:
'*Keep it simple*, lads, jist keep it simple…'

*For Sir Jimmy Shand, MBE, MA, MD, etc. Extra-ordinary Band
Leader, Composer, Personality, who held the world in awe for over
seventy years. Alasdair Catto-Shearer.*

IN
LOVING MEMORY
OF
SIR JIMMY SHAND M.B.E. M.A.
DIED 23rd DECEMBER 2000
AGED 92 YEARS
BELOVED HUSBAND
OF
LADY ANNE SHAND
AND A DEVOTED DAD AND GRANDAD

HAPPY TO MEET SORRY TO PART
HAPPY TO MEET AGAIN

SHAND

PENMAN

Author's 'reflection' is accidentally on the memorial, ironically as in the book title

*Author next to the newly unveiled bronze of Sir Jimmy Shand
September 2004*

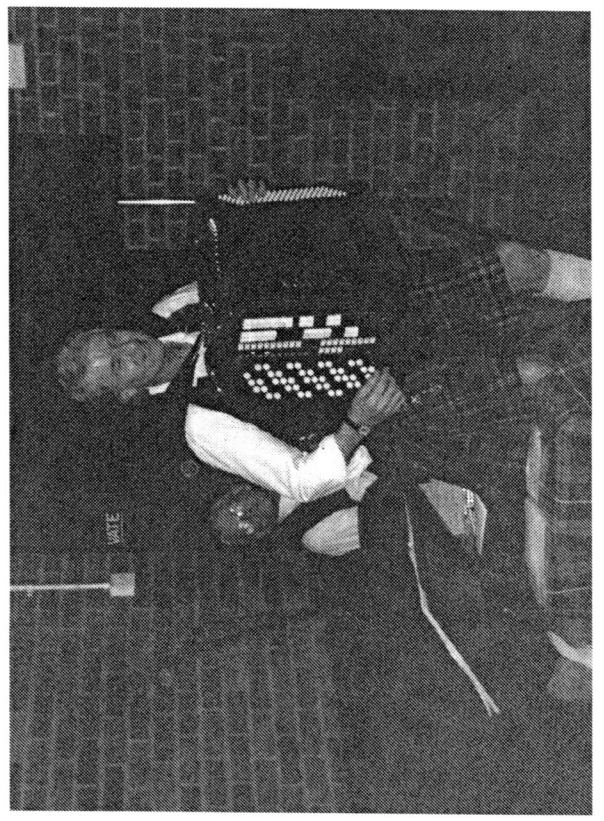

Author's personal tribute to Sir Jimmy Shand, 'Soldier on Jim Lad', December 2000

The Soldier's Farewell

Lyrics by Ally Shearer, 10 May 2005.
To Sandy and Sheena Laing's Waltz by Robbie McCombie.

Last night as I stood all alone by the sea,
A young soldier was marching away, far away,
A brave soldier lad, with his young face so sad –
To his sweetheart these words he did say:

Chorus:

'As we roamed through the fields and the valleys below,
Where we both fell in love, you and I –
Where you taught me to love you, dear Molly adored –
Now teach me to bid you goodbye.'

And if I should fall in the battle my love,
And what more can a brave soldier do –
My last dying words will be Molly – adieu,
To my Mother, my Country and you.

Chorus: repeat.

The Sounds o' Scotia

Composed by Ally Shearer, Wednesday, 8 November 2006.
A Song; Begins: D Major, 3/4 time.

Home once again, tae the sounds that I love,
The sweetest of sounds, fit for heav'n above.

The Question

Composed by Ally Shearer, 14 February 2005, at 3 a.m.

If there's a sacred heart for me,
To do the things I do,
The same will come – and to ensure
That I'll return to you;
For in life's lonely treasure spent
In searching for a love,
It sure is sweet, perhaps to meet,
For the power of all – is love.

The Teuchters' 'Simmer' Ball

*Composed by Ally Shearer, 22 May 2006, at 9.30 p.m. Reworded
24 May 2006, at 12.45 a.m.*

*(I have found in England they're clever as ever – so here's some
clever 'Scotch' for ye.)*

(Ad-lib style, in Doric.)
Song; tune adapted from 'Jeely Pigs'! (Key, C Major to be noted.)

Noo there wis Ivy Reid, fae Peterheid,
And loons frae up the 'Broch',
Wi' Sam McCall fae Whinney – 'Faul',
A' sweemin' in the loch,
Syne Newry loon fae Turra' toon –
Behavin' kinda roch,
Whin Jim and Maud fae Tillymaud –
Cam' doon tae jyne the fun.

Music, two lines.

Then Jerry's Dad wis awfy glad,
The music hud begun,
Till Geordie Sangster's 'Tackity beets',
Pit a'body on the run!
Then puir auld sod, the midden trod –
Like he was in the churn
As Bill and Andy hud enuff,
And fell inside the burn.

Mou' music and box – whole verse.

Then Waddy Watson dunced aroon.
The gerls 'e fairly gott'em,
Till 'e tummilt doon inside the loch,
And sank richt tae the bottem,
Then half a doz'n efter him
Ye never wida' thot'em!
Till up Wad pop't an' fisht'em oot,
He saved 'em every wan –
An ilkie-wan wis sober
Like before they hid begun.

So – thon's the kinda' capers.
That we a' gorrupte then
But worse things happint efter that,
Awa beyon' oor ken –
Better fun than a' the rest.
On Sunday efter tea,
Wis when it com' tae lovin' time.
For Ivy Reid and me.

The Wee Boy in His 'Jim-Jams'
(Rubbing his eyes, by the window)

Composed by Ally Shearer, 16 July 2006.
Key F (for Song, or part of).

There's a gentle little breeze
Comin' wafting thru' the trees.
As I stand here in me jammys in the mornin';
But if it's all the same tae you,
And you know I'm only two,
An' I am sleepy as an owl,
So don't be scornin'.

The Wee Divil

*In the Scottish rhymin' vernacular – a humorous poym; related to a
true incident in 1952.*
Composed by Ally Shearer, 30 January 2006, 6.30–6.40 p.m.
Key, F Major, if to be sung.

There was a man, an awfu' bumptious man,
Related tae the 'Divil' – since he was in a pram.
He used tae grin at Mither, sayin', 'Rock me if you can –
Ah'm a cousin to the "Divil" – and am *st-ronger* than a
    man!'

One day at school time, he drove the master mad,
Who haud at last to wallop 'im, 'cause 'e was awfu' bad.
Next thing then, his sister – she got awfu', awfu' sad,
Sobbin', 'What-d'ye-wante'-bash 'im for? E's jist a little lad
    – Awe! Awe!'

Noo this young 'Divil', seein' this, decides to go between,
An' jyne up wi' the weakest, for that was aye his scene.

Noo the very next thing that happened, when he was
    seventeen,
He hog-tied up the Dominie, wi' laces fae his sheen,
An' he tied him tae the school gate – puir Dominie was
    afraid,
Tae hear the ringin' o' the bell: it was the fire brigade.
So the fire brigade they doused 'im, an' the knots they
    tightened up,
Man, they fairly weel de-loused 'im, but couldna' get-'im-
    up!

So! the bolt cutters, being handy, man, 'twis a sorry state.
Up inside the 'ambyelince', strapp't tae a rawt-irn gate!
And the 'hospiddle' engineered tae free puir Dominie's plight,
Ye cud fairly hear 'im rattlin', thru' the middle o' the night.

A-aye! Ayye! (Slowly, like Rhoda.)
Till the 'Divil' cam' and freed 'im, fae a' his troublin' chain,
Sayin', 'Dinna yoo strap my bairn, sir – or Ah'll be roon again!'

Repeat these two lines.

(Tune idea established.)

Thoughts on Composition/s During Welsh-Wales Travel September–October 2006

And particularly of the 'Travelling People', such as I've studied during thirty-six tours of Eire's twenty-six counties.

Composed by Ally Shearer, September 2006.

This soundproof 'tent', where I live in my mind,
All plastic bags and nothing to find,
'Roadside-teach' to the gypsies each,
Careful I am, never to preach.
For I know of the signs – *'No Travellers Here'*.
It's hugely 'our' loss – and there's little to fear,
For the gypsy heart, so solid and pure;
They have their day, okay, come the hour –
Manitas de Plata! He was the one,
At Royal Albert Hall – where they all stood as one –
A tiny soul with a tiny guitar,
And nephews and cousins all followed their star,
So remember 'de Plata' wherever you are,
For the Romany heart has travelled so far.

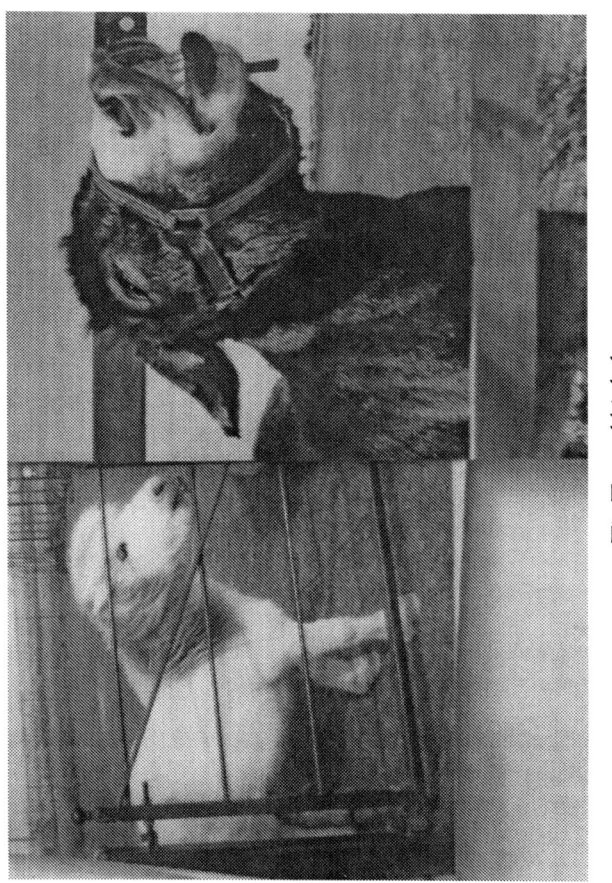

Tic-Tac and his lady
She reverts to the smug look, he to 'Huh! Like it or lump it, I'm off!'

Tic-Tac and his Lady

A 'tail' of a belligerent male donkey with his compadre – a female Shetland pony.

'Entitled' – From the Pear-shape to the Landscape – a Hundred Miles from Everywhere – Flat Across the Fens with Tic-Tac and his Lady.

*Description: She – white with brown mane (*The Boss*). He – Tic-Tac – colour black without* The Cross *on his back. Although he was never neglected and maltreated, as his* Lady *was, before being rescued. His main penchant in life is his dedication as a master escapologist for many miles over the Fens in search of 'girlfriends'… and so to their ode…*

She swings her head and a corner leg, to let him know
　　who's who,
Not made of Delft – 'tis she herself –
Who loves him through and through.
'Get out of that, you lousy rat, this is *my* carrot bowl!' –
And after all, 'tis him that's old, and she but a Shetland
　　foal,
Not skin and bone and far from home,
When her story'd first been told.

Thus domineering all the way, this sturdy fetlock stomps –
Yet still they canter through the hay –
Enjoy each other's romps.

They cannot speak, like we who speak,
Nor ask for love and care,
Their body lingo sez-it-all –
In even how they stare.
When stubbornness it is all gone,
And frolics they are few,
The donkeys and the ponies find nothing left to do.
But if we who strive, so they survive, continue in our
   quest,
Like Sue and Ken, just now and then –
Break even with the rest.
Blessed are they who know they are!

End.

A scribble of love.
From: Ally Shearer, composer of the above here, dated 5 August 2003,
7.20 to 7.30 p.m.

For Children in Need, Radio Cambridge.

Tipperty's Meg

(About a comical horse for my Heilan' brothers and sisters.)

Composed by Ally Shearer, 16 February 2005, at 3 a.m.

Tipperty's Meg had a broken leg,
So she couldnae gang tae the market,
She couldnae get far tae jump that bar,
Fair foonert and never got started.

Now she would've took the car
An' Seoris is awa, tae the roup –
On days like these, it's jist takin' the wheeze!
It's enough tae gar an auld horse loup.

Noo Meg she thunk, and she thunk, and – thunk!
And the leg was fairly yarket –
Had she louped that bar and traivilled by a car,
Weel, she couldnae very weel park it!

Noo Meg got sae bored, so she slept and she snored,
And she dreamed o' her loss in the 'rake-off' –
She awoke wi' a start, and a really huge (*mighty expiration of
    the windys*)
Syne she clears her throat, wi' a puff a' smoke
And – thocht… shi'd found – *vertical take-off*!

(It's finished soon…)
Then Meg she got cold, so she rolled and – she rolled
A' o'er the place in the dark,
At the end o' her stint, there wis a – gey – stink
An' the dogs on the place a' did bark!

(There's mair o' yon mare – Och aye!)
Noo the end wis nigh, for oor Meggie forby.
An' her spite got so *oh – very* bold.
She would trundle doon the hill
An' her snort was fit to kill,
An' the next twa words are *old* and *sold*! – (Terrible, eh?)

Noo I miss her yet, my lang-faced pet,
But ye ken weel, she *was* nearly deen,
And I've seen her yestreen, in auld Aiberdeen –
Her double… imagine how ye'd feel!

We wir twenty yairds apart,
And she pulled yon bachled cart
But I couldnae but see she had nae sheen –
(Aaaahhh!) – Sure it must a' been her foal
That was queuing for the dole,
An' tae think that Meg her Mither wis my queen!

Tipperty's Meg – alas! – Amen.
And apology tae ony person withoot a smile on the dole Q.

To a Legacy
(Is That a Leg Ah See?)

Composed by Ally Shearer, 14 October 2006.

A bench 'neath a Rowan or a Holly Tree
Is all they'll need to leave for me –
Where the tiny birds can all feel free
And the kindly folks may sit by me,
For Ally Shearer's RIP.

To Arvo and Annette – a Daughter

To the tune of 'Mattie's Song', F or G. Not original, adapted from memory.

From the window watch her go.
Head held high and hair a-blow,
The shoulder bag and swaying hips,
Down the garden path she trips,
Confidence in very stride,
Eager for the world outside,
With laughing face and waving hand,
She looks the finest in the land.

How she'd laugh if she could see,
Silly sentimental me,
Standing here all dewey-eyed,
Watching her with love and pride,
Thanking God, who did afford,
A humble man such rich reward:
A golden girl to call his own,
As time goes by, and on and on.

Music, two lines. Repeat all of verse two.

My daughter Annette; hubby Arvo; and, otherwise occupied, their daughter, Erin Nicole

To Be Alive

Composed by Ally Shearer, 28 March 2005, in a week of sunshine at noon – a thought (on such a day).

To be alive, on days like these
And just to laze, all in a daze, in the Summer haze
Is time enough to see
And remember the 'endless' country time
Which felt reserved for me
Days so long and spirit strong
When passions all ran free.

To Main Desk Diary/Visitors' Closure Book

(On leaving yet another homely farmstead and long-established Pottery Centre in West Wales.)

Composed by Ally Shearer, September 2006.

Superlatives and clichés all just go –
Around and round, and I'm finding all my 'needful *to* says'
Right now can not be found,
And so a simple thank you is all that I can say.
For this Highland heart feels better now,
So I must be on my way.

Signed, A S C Shearer.
PS: I've no erroneous views now! – Farewell – AS.

To My Own Sweet Lorraine
In Wendover, Ontario

Composed by Ally Shearer, end of August 1997, by Carrauntoohil,
'neath the huge black CO' Kerry Mountain.

Thinking of you much, and glad of your 'Back to College Efforts', and
all love to you and your 'Geordie', with little 'dancing girl' Connie.
Take care, practise stillness and calm. Love Dad xx.

Oh, what is rare as a day in June,
When, if ever, come perfect days?
Then Heaven tries the Earth, if it ever be in tune,
And over it her warm ear lays;
Whether we look, or whether we listen,
We hear life murmur, or see it glisten…
Now the heart is so full – that a drop over – fills it.
We are happy now, the Great God wills it.
For, no matter how barren the past may have been,
'Tis enough for us now, that the future looks green.

Perhaps it's truly in solitude all great thoughts are born.

To the Druid 'Hawk', Muso of Devon

Composed by Ally Shearer, Tuesday, 5 September 2006.

No mice, no moths in van life,
An' 'in perpetuity' all around outside
The sights and sounds – of wildlife,
The elements – 'What elements?' replied 'The Hawk',
Who also has inherited a thirteenth-century Sidford
cottage
All beamed and strutted, with obvious rafters in view
That came from the broken ships –
Which, before reclamation, sailed a mile 'inland'
From the mouth of the River *Sid*,
And where only a stout shingle slope
Has ever served as a 'harbour'
For the three fishing boats of today.

*NB: 'The Hawk' is a musical pal (untutored – banjo and guitarist) –
a poet of my English Folk Festival era. He is the High Devon and
Avebury Druid, in charge of Druid security in their 'House of Lords'
appearances on several occasions. The gifted son of a Romany father
(self-taught pianist, in high places, Europe etc.), who first inherited the
medieval cottage, in mid-Victorian times.*

To the Lasses o' Pont Street

Composed by Ally Shearer, 14 December 2004, a.m.

So, fareweel, ye Lass o' Bon Accord,
The Eightsome and the Reel,
Tae you the one, the special one,
I know just how ye feel.
The times we've known – my, how we've grown –
In stature and in dance.
Where e'er ye be on land or sea –
In France they dance The Dance.

Thru' all the years of love and pain
We danced perchance to joy sustain
When workday chores are done –
We're here again to pleasure fun,
Where we'll hae cheer wi' nought tae fear
Thru' all life's drawl disdain –
The bell o' St Columba doth ring for us again.

So when I'm gone, let dance go on.
As in the years of yore –
The Chelsea Reel and Highland Club –
McCluskey knew the score.
Three decades and some more they tell,
When Laurie's style began –
Resound within, the happy din –
A world as if one man.

Then came the time that cometh,
Tae a' creatures, great and small
The RSCDS took o'er the 'shop' and yet –
That isn't all!
That skill and dedication *can*, be social after all,
The *joie de vivre* o' dance perchance,
Doth vibrate any hall.

To the Music Makars Awa

Ally C Shearer, February 2003.

Abune thon trees on Trossach's hill,
Dwell memories that linger still,
O' magic sounds o'er glen and rill,
Sheer music overall.

Who knows where goes a gift like thine,
Fond legacy so mighty fine,
That spans the years through fingers new,
Could there be again, some lads like you?

Somewhere abune the cloud so fair,
'Tis sure there's yet a bygone player,
Who paints the stars wi' music rare,
For a' eternity.

So come, ye lads and lasses grand,
Mak 'em dance throughout the land,
There's skirl and dirl at your command,
For Starr, MacLeod, Gow, Skinner, Shand.

Somewhere I know they're listening still,
O'er island, glen and Croy's sweet hill,
So let them hear your spirit sound,
As we sing and dance the world around.

By way of a 'Testimonial' to the Music Makars here and gone.
As recited on BBC radio Scotland's 'The Reel Blend, with Robbie
Shepherd'

Author and partner with friends
Birling at centre in the dance, 'The Duke of Perth'
Berkhamsted, Herts 51st Annual Highland Ball, 2003

Traivilled

Composed 12 July 2005, at 4.30 a.m.

Noo some folks dae traivil tae broaden the mind,
Some'll hae traivil'd a fortune to find;
Some traivil'd far an' others far less,
An' there's those that aye feenish up, in a mess.
But me I began, wi' ma heid in a spin,
Tae try and discover the muddle within,
For graftin' much, dancin' some, playin' forby,
Tae imagine contentment – wis tellin' a lie;
So I traivil'd yon train, curled up on the shelf,
Peculiar direction – for findin' oneself.
Come Jan'ry '06 'twill be fifty years on –
Yet somehow I've known I wis never alone
So grateful this while, and jist council the years,
And worry nae mair – o' the tears and the fears.

Ally Shearer. Some birthday thoughts.

Traivilin' (1956–2006)

Composed by Ally Shearer, 17 March 2005.

My dearest cousin called me (20 March 2005), 6½ hours on the land-line. 'Twas a set-up, plotted the week before. Maybe we last spoke about 1953 – it's hard to say.

Weel, I've traivil'd much in Ireland and been to Aiberdeen,
Wi' mem'ries o' sic happy days and catapultin' stein,
Gull-eggin' doon bi' Bullers, whar Bram Stoker hud bin
seen;
Syne skivin' roon ahin' the stooks… wi' a pal ca'd Andy
Cheyne.
(So he learnt the Hohner Vamper – tho' drummin' was his
scene.)

Noo fairmin' wis oor happy life, and neebors were oor
frien's.
The Kennedys and Simons, dancin' roon wi' sonsie deems.
The Carnies and the Sangsters – thon time was fit for
dreams –
There'd be twenty roon the table, tattie-howkin wi' their
speens
(Like heowin's never-endin' queue, just strugglin' thru'
wir teens.)

'Course I was born – far too late, and never went to war –
Bare knee-caps swingin' on a gate, and searching – for my star,
I'd listen to the ripplin' burn, the buzzin' o' the bees –
And the wafflin' o' McGonnigle wid drive ye tae yer knees.
(We hud wallfloer an' sweet marigold, our mainly Summer
host –
But the mile-high swingin' tree-hoose – wis the joy we
loved the most.)

Atween a' thon I traivil'd in tae Peterheid's 'blue toon',
For Curly Allen's chanter, an' me – 'The Buchan Loon',
I'd bike it by the Lido – where the Warders learnt tae box
And the burglar 'John Raminsky' gar'd me pu' up ma sox
(I smelt fermintin' whisky as I gethered up ma speed;
Tho' I never saw my sweetheart, golden lovely Ivy Reid.)

Syne efter that, I left the place, where once I went tae
school.
The Academy and Port Errol – where I often played the
fool!
Tho' I'd never dwelt inside it – my first toon o' Peterheid,
And how I rued the pairtin' wi' my darlin' Ivy Reid.
(So – on the run – my life begun, for England on a train
How I pondered – and I wondered – wid I e'er see hame
again?)
But now I know that I will go, and struggle up yon hill;
Which served me perfect mem'ry agin' mony a Winter's
chill.
(Well, a man's allowed to dream; and besides, the savage
loves his native shore – an' that's a fact.)

In the frosty January, pummelled Caterham Barrack
square,
Thru' Winter's blast oor time rush't past – I wisht I wasnae
there!
But the love of a vocation was, for some other few.
And tae gain a learnin' process – whit wis a lad to do?
(But duck and dive – fecht and strive – an' jist learn a thing
or two!)
My trusty auld melodyin' wis ayewis by my side
Like my wee sma' Brownie cam'ra – there wis no place to
hide!
So I've traivil'd on manoeuvres and dug in the world aroon
And the lads wid a' start singin' – when they heard the Ally
soond –
(Aye, the lads wid a' start singin' when they'd hear young
Ally's tune.)

So – happy to meet, an' sorry to part –
Army days and affairs o' the heart,
Brigs they're a' burned – banished the fears,
My sweetheart she has called me, after nearly fifty years!
Noo there's coontless hours, that we hae spent, oorsel's
    upon the phone!
It's easy-peasie seein' now – I never wis alone
For 'twas no weary journey we hae traivil'd in between…
(Tho' half a hunder years ago, I left auld Aiberdeen –
And I must'a' worn oot aboot a thoosan' pair o' sheen.)

Arbuthnott, Aberdeenshire, December 2005–January 2006

Tribute to Diana, the People's Princess

As inserted in the Condolence Book, Harrods, by Ally Shearer,
September 1997.

The mirror's truth, you need not fear,
As from your youth you sever.
The beauty that you shared with us,
Will be with us for ever.

Troubled Times

Composed by Ally Shearer, 14 August 2005.

There are a million bicycles in Beijing,
The state of the world we're living in –
Is there any decent song, that they can sing
To renew the hell the world is all in?

People are the trouble don't you see.
For there's nothing wrong at all with the you and the me.
We like to imagine a world safe and free,
With true joie de vivre, on land or on sea.

So what's the cure for our planetary ails?
After all, it's just people who bring about wails.
It's not melting ice caps – or killing the whales,
To seek evolution – just read Darwin's tales.

With hi-tech for living, all under the sky,
Hi-tech for funerals, whenever you die.
Hi-tech has banished the working man's eye –
No longer employed in fields full of rye!

Tsunamis Come
(Wi' some Political Satire) in truth

Composed by Ally Shearer, 31 January 2005.

Tsunamis come, as tsunamis go,
People – help the story flow,
When she comes, nobody knows,
But no heed of the overflow.

'Frisco's bridge came tumbling down,
Catastrophic news – sped the world around
Soon was found – in a comfy office – on higher ground,
'How could there be a crack below –
Two miles or so of ocean flow?'

'Rebuild it higher on double deck!'
Some simple minds suggest,
For higher the flyer,
Takes longer to fall:
Time alone will stand the test!

Brains to kick is what they've got,
To aid the sufferers' plightful lot
To take command of Outer Space –
'We'll save the planet and the human race' – (sez The
    Bush!)

The 'educated' scoff at the ozone layer,
And blank it out – 'For it isn't there!'
'Our fossil fuel, we've always had' –
So it's head down, plough on,
'Who gives a damn for old Baghdad?'

'*Their* affairs are all their own,
And all we have is all home-grown…
The Taliban can stay at home.
They should know we do no wrong.'

'*We* who love our Western ways,
Don't care how these folks wend their ways
We spend "ours" in our smoke-filled haze.
And in between there's land to raze' –
So to avoid *their* system's 'clever' craze.

'We can't live *theirs*, and they not *ours*,
For us it's easier to just grow flowers –
We can't save their millions' –
In long unholy slight: 'Best they only – keep it out of
    sight.'

The consolation found in prayer,
When there's life worthwhile and no table bare –
Too well informed can be ill informed,
But peace on earth becomes more and more – rare.

'U-hoo, I'm on the Loo!'

(Not a tough one to imagine, which maybe should've been the title –
Imagine!)

Composed by Ally Shearer, Saturday, 15 July 2006 (Yon time).
Tune, Killybegs; Key, F.

Now there's something that I do,
When I'm sitting on the loo
And it happens all-of-a-sudden without warning:
I just drop-off fast asleep,
Till-from-my-dream I take a leap,
Up off me 'twilit' seat, into the dawning…
Imagine!

Verses From My Early Life

Memorised like the Desiderata for a Charity Concert. (They called it a 'Benefit Show'. I felt this to be an appropriate title.)

Ally Shearer, after midnight, 29 November 2006.

God Bless all sick folk everywhere.
And all who suffer pain
All invalids and crippled folk,
And all who long have lain
In bed by day and night, and know,
How wearily the hours go.
God Bless all those who love these folk.
And have them in their care,
Who bravely minister to them
And all their weakness share;
God give them strength, the weak to bless,
And help them in their helplessness.

Waltzing Forever With You

Music and lyrics by Ally Shearer – 23 July 2002.
Arranged by Ally Shearer and Flora McCrae.

Wherever you are I'm following you
Wherever you go I'm going there too
Whatever you feel I'm feeling for you
And I'm waltzing forever with you.

However you are, however I'll be,
Somewhen, somewhere so plainly I see
The reason you're there is waiting for me
And I'm waltzing forever with you.

So now that I know where Heav'n's for me
There's someplace I go where no one can see
And the winning and losing means nothing to me
Just as long as you're singing with me.

My song tribute for the late Will Starr, world famous musical entertainer.

Waz It? Iz It?

Tuesday, 18 November 2003, early a.m.

Have we been here before?
Have we travelled through this door
On our way to nothing more?
Is your heart still feeling sore,
And are you lonely too?
No more for me and you,
Is there nothing left to view?
Are we both so drab and blue –
That we haven't got a clue?
Just living once again, tho' never homely,
This life with us apart, existing only.

Wendover Woods

Composed by Ally Shearer, Friday, 3 November 2006.
Song – tune composed 8 November 2003; Key, F Sharp Major.

Will you walk, love, now with me,
By the sweet hills near the sea?
Let us find our winding stream,
Where we loved and shared our dream.

In the woods, dear, so free,
Darling, come one more time with me,
By the sunset o'er the lea
And our path winds home to me.

Band in and duet hums tune – last two lines, verse one.

Will you walk home with me,
By our neat hills beside the sea?
In the woods, dear, by our stream,
Where we loved and shared our dream.

What Matters

Composed by Ally Shearer, September 2006.

True friendship, honesty and love –
Remembering the Desiderata;
And always, that the most wasted of *all* days
Is one without laughter.
And if you see someone without a smile
Give them one of yours.

The Author in humorous song, with a full house 'at home' in Scotland, Easter 2002

Where Are We Going?

Composed by Ally Shearer, 30 March 2003.

Where are we going? – We thought we knew.
But now we're not so sure...
We lost our way in the crazy maze...
Now searching for a cure.

We can't go on:
It's back to turn – to seek
The wisdom of the past;
Hard lessons to relearn.

Back to the light that guided us
When we were great and glorious;
Back to the old morality
For the mighty spirit over us.

Where My Highland River Flows

Composed by Ally Shearer, 16 November 2004.
Key, C; tune, traditional (adapted).

Intro – last line.

There's a pretty spot so Highland,
I always claim for my land,
Where the heather and the bonnie broom
Will never, never die.
It's the land of the fine ceilidh,
My heart goes back there daily,
To the girl I left behind me,
When we kissed and said 'Goodbye'.

Chorus:

Where my dear old river's flowing,
Where the purple heather's growing,
Where my heart is, I am going –
To my little Highland rose.
And the moment that I meet her,
With a hug and kiss I'll greet her,
For there's ne'er a lassie sweeter,
Where my Highland river flows.

There's no letter I'll be mailing,
For soon will I be sailing,
And I'll bless the ship that takes me,
To my dear old Highland shore.
There I'll settle down for ever,
I'll leave my homeland never,
And I'll whisper to my sweetheart,
'Stay with me for evermore...'

Chorus repeat, plus last line.
(Tune in book.)

View River Spey between Grantown and Tomintoul

Where to Now?

Composed by Ally Shearer, 27 March 2003.
Song probably 3/4 time.

So where are you now, and do you recall,
The soul-wrenching day by the old castle wall?
How sweet was our sorrow, as the warm tears did fall,
And they welcomed the earth, in her embracing shawl.
This long time has passed and I still see your face.
With your laughter and song all over the place.

Tell me... is there some truth in existence at all?
Or are you the dream, I forever recall?
Does the God in his Heaven consider us when
Between here and there we just meet – now and then?

If life must be trouble 'tween lovers and friends.
Through joys of fond meetings – to parting again.
Together, what purpose do we share so dear,
When all questions answered and nothing to fear?

So if our farewell – be fantasy too –
How worth would life be, were there nothing but you?
There's much to inspire us, as we struggle through,
And lapse in the dreamtime – of somewhen and you.

Whose Island Anyway?

Composed by Ally Shearer, 14 December 2006, at midnight.

Now, I'm not an island – so what about you?
With affairs of the heart – so what's there to do?
All happy to meet and sorry to part,
But what's there to do, with affairs of the heart?

Bin Laden, he feels that the West ain't too smart,
As he trains up *Al-Qaeda* to blow us apart,
Yet for all of his dreams, and Hitler-like schemes,
The one with his name on – will part all the seams.

Still, with our big four-by-fours, and our jammed-up
    school runs,
No exercise time for beleaguered Mums,
Drugs we accept, from Afghanistan –
Good neighbours we keep, from old Pakistan…

Plenty to eat, and fun things to do,
But what of a 'Life' – for me and for you?
More mosques to build for prayer all day long,
A country was ours – but won't be for long…

Christmas will come – don't let us be bombed,
How is it I feel somehow we are wronged?
But I'll solve it for me, and it won't take me long,
Departing the place, I had conquered in song.
Yes, I'll head for the North, and it won't take me long.

Good years, full bent on giving it all –
And no giving way – when pressed to the wall!
What's it all for, in the *great after-all*?
Are others so bright – are we really that *small*?

But if greatness be ego – there's need to forestall,
For ego and greed are not greatness at all,
Else, again and again, must true greatness fall!
It's the end, it's the end – for us all, for us all.

NB: Perhaps thoughts too sombre for a culmination to 2006... AS.

Wildlife

Composed by Ally Shearer in the neep field, Arbuthnott, Aberdeen-shire, on 2 January 2006.

Twa thousan' craws risin' and restin',
Somewhile noo, before the nestin',
Neep field a-plenty an' mair tae spare,
An' a' is free – 'cause there's naebody there.
Sunshine's warm, tho' the frost is hoar,
Hing aroon and Ah'll tell ye more…
Yin mair mile to 'Bervie toon,
Ah've writ' a' this jist walkin' aroon.

With Reference to 'The Exiled Scot'

Composed by Ally Shearer, Tuesday, 29 August 2006, along with dog in sunshine bliss.

With added reference to Sir John Betjeman, 100 years on – 28 August 2006.

The exiled Scot sees nothing to fear, little to gain, nothing
    too queer,
As he scribbles down thoughts, through the mundane year.
After all, he's just a *'wee exile'*.

But an exile style can be sometimes best
Or the exile while, no better than the rest
Seeks identity yet, with a lifelong past,
No reason *then*, maybe, to be nailed to the mast
Of a work-life mode, simply saving for the 'last'.

So ignore 'im if you will, ignore 'im if you must,
It's hardly a crime, to be pure and just,
But a man signed Robin – a *worldwide Burns*,
Heeded less the ignorance – as bigots took their turn.
They scribbled without rhyme, their ridicule and scorn,
Well past the time *Rabbie Burns'* fame was born.

And it happens yet today – not that God alone knows,
As the *Oxford Book* shows – without rhyme, it's only prose.
So well done, Mr Betjeman – so capable of both.
In his narrative also, your humour he could clothe.

So the humble and the simple, of the poets who are
    blessed,
And contemporaries gone, soon buried wi' the rest,
With an *amen* – and yes, a deep respect for –
'A man's a man for a' that!'

With Thoughts of the Bullers of Buchan

Also these words, composed on 20 March 2004.

Yon happy days, sae far back noo…
Roon Sodger Cowie's forge,
We loved tae gether mushrooms
Doon by the Bullers Gorge.

I'd staun and stair at your red hair.
Admirin' frae afar,
As fresh as ony daisy,
Ye twinkled like a star,
At twelve year old, and none so bold,
Jist wundrin' what you are!

Pure bashfu' as could be,
Perplexed, I'd wonder
How this big toon girl
Could ever fancy me?
As ye'd lean aginst yer Aunty's door.
And send my heart a-twirl,
And my nearly-brain was lost – back then,
Ye knew what you could furl.

Sae far from my world o' country things,
'Twis ayewis you – and oh, by jings! –
I'm on my bike and my young heartstrings
Go pedallin' mad and loudly sings!
It's an empty satisfaction
Just to wander round and round,
Just knowing in my heart of hearts,
You're nowhere to be found.

Noo I think of you, some days it's true,
Returned to simple life,
Unnoticed in my goings,
Unpossessing of a wife.
I sit alone, though not alone –
As oft-times done before –
Must I for ever lean against –
This ever open door?

Why Do We Love?

Composed by Ally Shearer, 31 January 2003.

Why do we love in the Springtime so fair?
Why do we love in the Fall?
Why do we love the birds of the air?
Oh, why do we love at all?

And why do we care if there is nobody there –
No one to take to the ball?
And why do we smile, alone all the while?
Why do we smile at all?

Why in the sunshine do you glow like wine?
Why do I, when you call?
Why do I glow in the Wintertime
With you nowhere near me at all?

Why do I feel so, that life is worthwhile,
With only these thoughts to recall?
And why do we kiss in a soft evening mist,
When my heart is in your hand so small?

Just give me your hand and we'll walk down the Strand,
Through daylight or darkness and squall,
Alone here I stand, with your heart in my hand,
Dear Lord, am I dreaming at all?

Have I no pride that flows like the tide,
To keep me upright should I fall?
How can I heal all this hurting inside,
And why do I love you at all?

Repeat last two lines.

NB: Also an early song for John Wright.

Years 2000 – and Questions

Composed by Ally Shearer, 21 May 2006, twelve noon.

All life so pressured, massed with care,
No benefit of time, for pleasures stare
With annihilation on the go,
Since Taliban ordained it so.
Are *we* so wrong in our happy state?
Must *we* to other realms relate?
So many *wars* – more lost than won –
What now, of awful deeds all done?

Is payback time the tomorrow's 'now'?
Who was it started the longest – row?
Three nations pillaged all the rest.
Must we all now just do *our* best
To keep the Jealous Wolf at bay,
And watch our Planet's fast decay?
If there were powers from way above
Decreeing the *Answer* to be love,
Wise men would rule and the greedy fall,
For love to conquer over all.

You
To Colleen – a Granddaughter

Composed by Ally Shearer, 23 February 2006.
Song?

I now can see the cry and hue,
But never mind events tae rue –
Just hold your lovely head on high,
And think of me – as you go by;
What e'er you see that 'they' can do,
What e'er troubles do ensue,
Do what only *you* can do
And the Mighty World will turn with you.

The Author and bonnie Colleen Chartrand, daughter of his Lorraine,
Wendover, Ontario and Surrey County, England

Young Man's Dream of Edin' O'er
(A less than happy time, told with flippancy)

Composed by Ally Shearer, 20 October 2004.

I strode to Edinburgh, once imagined – 'O' sic reverie!'
From years of postcards, pictures, dance – to '87 or '93.
Thenceforth I sprang from London town –
Decamping train and feeling free,
My happy spirit did abound,
'Mid smokeless jostling – Waverley.

Emerging from my nine-hour night,
A sight I thought to never see
Bravely into morning light –
This toon o' Edinburgh – there! At last for me.

This dream-town, castle on a hill,
The cobbled walks, all fancy-free –
Yet I'd not land agin' my will,
Sae far awa as infancy.

The trudge I made, that silly time.
Thru' that great place, of dreams sublime,
Rain, wind and hail did undermine –
My youthful – dim – expectancy,
My feeling now, sae far from fine –
Just me and grim 'ad-varsity'…

…of life that is – thru' wait and see –
Till spiral stairway softly climb
To luxury – of, a B & B.

'Twas little wunner – 'Jim's' remark –
On spying tiny honeypot –
Wi' forethought o' musician's lot,
Yet grateful some, for a' they got –
Said, 'Ma'am, I see ye keep a bee.'*

'And there's more!'

That said, there was me,
Oot o' ma depth, and up a gum tree.
I said to myself, 'I'll never be free.'
She's roon Cairngorm, lookin' for me.
But *I'm* staying put – Archie Fisher to see
'Cause the closeness of my kind is where I need to be,
Wi' the Culture I'm inherent – it's the only way for me.

---

* Courtesy of the family of the late Sir Jimmy Shand.

Princes Street Gardens, Edinburgh Castle

You – Whoever You Are!

Composed by Ally Shearer, Thursday, 9 March 2006, at 2.15 a.m.

How much longer to wait around for you,
How much more to sit around and stew?
Seems to be it's all for you, and nothing else for me.
You need a fool to sit and wait, compromise and contemplate
You're supercilious run around with all the different guys
    in town.

But then in truth you must be you –
To-be-born-at-all, in truth be true
To thine own self, and gain what's due.
Thus live in reverie – beside your personal coded star –
Identifying who you are, never losing sight of this,
Nor where to plant the waiting kiss.

But what of shattered hearts behind.
Forgotten dreams to – 'never mind'
You cannot help the things you do,
Aren't 'you-the-one', with comely hue?
Maybe you're right to never care –
For them with whispering heads that stare,
There's love to own the fun you serve,
To what great honour, do they preserve?

And so must I no longer wait
For you upon this golden shore?
Nor lift you clean up off the sand,
To dance you round and round no more.
Nor hear delighted skirls of mirth,
From lips to once adore,
Those times sublime were yours and mine,
Those Summertimes galore. Amen to then!

A Personal Tribute to Astronomer/Scientist, Sir Patrick Moore
Ally Shearer, 05.30 hours, Monday 30 April, 2007

I wake up in the morning
With sunshine round my door,
And stumble to the bathroom
Along the creaking floor.
Loving every moment –
As if they were the last,
And relishing the memory
Of that Springtime gone so fast.

Much earlier than this time o'er,
The city dark and tame;
I gazed in awesome wonder
As if a boy again.
My heart it pounded wildly
As I visioned just one name,
Sir Patrick Moore of Selsey,
With some fifty years of fame;
And the tune that went,
Which was heaven-sent,
From beyond my window frame.

For no one else has struggled,
So long to keep us right
Through countless hours of scrutiny –
Revealing skies at night.
The forty years of interest, my humble time sustained,
Like many more, so gladly sure
That Patrick Moore remained,
To fill with joy, both man and boy
Such knowledge unsurpassed,
His self-taught science of the skies
Will last – and last – and last.

So now I feel I must explain
What started me this jot;
You see, it's never hard for me
When I've struggled from my cot;
Imagining the early sky,
Is a thing I like a lot…
And even tho' the sky-high planes
Be just a silver dot…
To me it seems, the evaporation streams
Are like the 'Flying Scot' –
O'er the Atlantic view, they several spew,
And, some-might-be Aeroflot…

Even today! As 'Cold War' looms once more.

Auld Lang Syne
By Robert Burns

Should auld acquaintance be forgot,
And never brought to mind?
Should auld acquaintance be forgot,
And auld lang syne?

Chorus:

For auld lang syne, my dear,
For auld lang syne,
We'll tak a cup o' kindness yet,
For auld lang syne.

And there's a hand, by trusty fiere!
And gies a hand o' thine!
A we'll tak a right gude-willie waught,
For auld lang syne.

Chorus:

For auld lang syne, my dear,
For auld lang syne,
We'll tak a cup o' kindness yet,
For auld lang syne.

Ard Choille Music for Auld Lang Syne

Glossary

A

a'	*all*
a'body	*everybody*
aboot	*about*
abos	*aboriginals*
abune	*above*
Achi'	*Achilles*
ach-tae	*oh to*
agin'	*against*
ahin'	*behind*
ain	*own*
airt	*where from*
alang	*along*
ah'm a' richt ye ken	*I'm all right you know*
apairt	*apart*
Ard Choille	*High Wood*
aroon	*around*
at a'	*at all*
a' tapa'	*on top of*
Auld Lang Syne	*long since gone*
auld	*old*
awa	*away*
awfy	*awful*
aye/ayewis	*always*

319

B

baith	*both*
bannox	*griddle cakes*
bi	*by*
bide	*stay or live*
bin	*been*
bogey	*animal feed or other cart*
Bon Accord	*Aberdeenshire*
bonnie	*beautiful*
bothy	*abode for single male farm workers*
briagha (Gaelic)	*beautiful*
broon	*brown*
bubbilee-Jox	*turkey cocks*
burra won't	*but I won't*

C

ca'd	*called*
cadger	*sponger*
ca'in'	*calling*
cam'	*come*
canna	*cannot*
cauld	*cold*
ceilidh	*Scottish traditional entertainment*
chanter	*mouth and finger piece of bagpipes*
chiel	*young man*
childer	*children*
claes	*clothes*
consensicle	*possible nonsense*

coo'	*cow*
cowrin'	*cowering*
craic (Irish Gaelic)	*the crack*
crake	*corncrake (bird)*
crowdy	*peopled*
cud	*could*
cudgel	*large wooden cosh*
cued mile fàilte (Scots Gaelic)	*hundred thousand welcomes*

D

dacent (Scots/Irish)	*decent*
dei'	*do/die*
deems	*young women*
deen	*done*
dinna	*don't*
dirge	*slow, sad*
dirl	*rapid movement e.g. staccato*
dochter	*daughter*
Dominie	*headmaster*
doon	*down*
dour	*stubborn*
drawl	*slow, dreary*
dreichy	*drab, wet*
dug (some areas)	*dog*
dunce	*dance*
duncin'	*dancing*

E

echty	*eighty*
e'e	*eye*
eez	*his*
enuff	*enough*
ey	*always*

F

fae/frae	*from*
fair bikin'	*really cycling*
fairmin'	*farming*
fa's feel-are-ee	*whose fool are you*
faun	*when*
fecht	*fight*
feenish'd	*finished*
fender	*hearth*
fe-ye	*from you*
fleer	*floor*
floers	*flowers*
foonert	*tired*
frien'	*friend*
fu'	*full*
furl	*whirl*
furlin'	*whirling*
fu'r ye dein	*how are you doing?*
futterin'	*running feet sound (NE Scotland)*

G

gaird'n	*garden*
galorum	*plentiful*
gan'	*gone/going*
gars	*makes*
gei's	*give us*
gel	*girl*
getya, letya	*get you, let you*
gin'	*if, by*
Glesca	*Glasgow*

glint	*gleam*
gloamin'	*twilight*
greetin'	*crying*
grockles	*city holiday folk*
guddle	*stand in water and catch by hand (e.g. river eels)*
guid	*good*
gull-eggin'	*collecting seagulls' eggs*

H

hae	*have*
hae'en	*having*
hairt	*heart*
hairst	*harvest*
hames	*homes*
havenae	*have not*
hauds	*holds*
haud yer weesht	*be quiet*
haun	*hand*
heids	*heads*
Heilan'	*highland*
helistergowdy	*head over heels*
heowin	*hoeing*
heuch	*howe/ravine*
hing	*hang*
hombre (Spanish – impolite)	*man*
hud	*had*
hunder	*hundred*
hurl	*throw*

I

ither	*other*
ilka wan 'os	*every one of us*

J

jiggin'	*dancing*
jim-jams/jammys	*pyjamas*
jist	*just*
jyne	*join*

K

ken	*know*
kerried	*carried*
kin	*can*
kith and kin	*relatives*
knowes	*glens (Scots)*

L

laffin'	*laughing*
lang	*long*
lauch	*laugh*
lave o't	*rest of it*
leppin	*leaping*
licht	*light*
lo'e	*love*
loon (NE Scot)	*boy/young man*
loups	*jumps*
lousin'	*stopping; finishing*

M

M1	*first motorway*
mair	*more*
'mang	*among*
michty	*mighty*
midden	*manure heap*
mony	*many*
moochin'	*sniffing around*
mo-oucha (Baranya, Hungary)	*mother*
morra'	*tomorrow*
mou'	*mouth*
muckle	*big/many*
muckle mair	*many more*
mune	*moon*
Myn' fa yer-bappin', tee-to uppa-ginst	*mind who you are bumping up against*

N

nae doot	*no doubt*
neebor	*neighbour*
neeps	*turnips*
nip-off	*hop over/away*
nite	*night*

O

och	*oh*
o'er	*over*
oor	*our*
oot	*out*
owt	*anything else*

P

pairtin'	*parting*
plaid (pronounced 'plaad')	*Tartan shoulder shawl*
ploo'	*plough*
praties (Irish)	*potatoes*
Polis	*police*
pooches	*pockets*
prood	*proud*
pu'	*pull*
puir	*poor*

Q

quaich	*Celtic drinking goblet*
quair	*queer, odd*
quine (NE Scot)	*girl*

R

raither	*rather*
rake o't	*rest of it*
regaled	*talked to*
roamin'	*roaming*
richt	*right*
rin	*run*
roch	*rough*
roon	*round*
roon the ben	*round the bend*
RSCDS	*Royal Scottish Country Dance Society*
rump and stot	*jump and bounce*
rye	*part of whisky content, makings*

S

sae	*so*
sark	*shirt*
scoots	*travel at speed*
scyowed	*squint*
Seturdi	*Saturday*
shebeen	*small home*
sheen	*shoes*
shied	*frightened*
sic	*such*
sicht	*sight*
simmer	*summer*
sine	*then*
skelping	*spanking*
skirl	*shriek*
skint	*broke*
skivin'	*shirking*
slanj'e var	*good health*
slurpin'	*drinking*
sma'	*small*
sna'	*snow*
sodger	*soldier*
sonsie	*buxom*
sook and blaw	*suck and blow*
soond	*sound*
sorra	*sorrow*
spean	*spoon*
speir	*ask*
spreadaggled	*spread out*
staunin'	*standing*

steins	*stones*
stooks	*propped on base corn sheaves*
stottin'	*bouncing*
strewn	*scattered*
sweemin'	*swimming*

T

tackity beets	*studded boots*
tae	*to*
tak	*take*
tattie-howkin	*potato digging*
teuch	*tough*
teuchits	*peeweep (bird)*
thoosan'	*thousand*
the gither	*together*
thole	*stand (put up with)*
thon	*yon (a remembered time)*
toon	*town*
thrashin'	*threshing, i.e. corn*
thristle	*thistle*
traivilled	*travelled*
trudging	*trekking*
tumblin'	*tumbling*
tummell	*tumble*
twa	*two*
twinty	*twenty (a score)*

U

uz	*us*

W

wa'	*wall*
wafflin'	*flannelling*
wail	*shout*
wark	*work*
watter	*water*
way up a 'kye (child speak)	*up in the sky*
weel kent	*well known*
wha	*who*
whan	*when*
whar/whaur	*where*
whurlaroon	*whirl around*
wid	*would*
wimna	*with me*
wi'	*with*
win's	*winds*
wint	*went*
wir	*we are*
wisnae	*was not*
wither	*weather*
wi've	*we have*
wiz	*was*
woodie	*wood pigeon*
wrang	*wrong*
wull	*will*
wundrin'	*wondering*
wunna	*wont*

wunner	*wonder*
wurds	*words*
wyte	*wait*

Y

yairds	*yards*
yer	*your*
yersel	*yourself*
yestreen	*yesterday evening*
yett	*gate*
yin	*one*
yokin'	*starting (work)*
youse	*you ones*
yumpin'	*jumping*

Index

Presentations at concert end for 'CHAS' Scotland
Author and Flora MacGregor with music pupils

Dear Valerie,

(Partaking in small liberty
of addressing thee; neat "courtesy"
In this reign Okay! – for it's only to me:
For after all – it's only to thee;
~ In gratitude) you bow without soliloquy.
For keep Lady O' the dance.
Fine

Aye happy to meet
Sorry to part's

Yours Aye,
(F)asdaic (Aly) S.C.
Stewart Pete,
11-11-
2007.

Printed in the United Kingdom
by Lightning Source UK Ltd.
123722UK00001B/19-30/A